The
Wanderer

The Wanderer

AN ALASKA WOLF'S FINAL JOURNEY

Tom Walker

MOUNTAINEERS
BOOKS

MOUNTAINEERS BOOKS is dedicated to the exploration, preservation, and enjoyment of outdoor and wilderness areas.

1001 SW Klickitat Way, Suite 201, Seattle, WA 98134
800-553-4453, www.mountaineersbooks.org

Printed in the United States of America
Distributed in the United Kingdom by Cordee, www.cordee.co.uk

26 25 24 23   1 2 3 4 5

Copyeditor: Sarah Breeding
Design and layout: Jen Grable
Maps: National Park Service
All photographs by the author unless credited otherwise
Cover images: Tom Walker

Library of Congress cataloging-in-publication data is available at https://lccn.loc.gov/2022043350. The ebook record is available at https://lccn.loc.gov/2022043351.

Mountaineers Books titles may be purchased for corporate, educational, or other promotional sales, and our authors are available for a wide range of events. For information on special discounts or booking an author, contact our customer service at 800-553-4453 or mbooks@mountaineersbooks.org.

This product is made of FSC®-certified and other controlled materials.

ISBN (paperback): 978-1-68051-613-5
ISBN (ebook): 978-1-68051-614-2

An independent nonprofit publisher since 1960

MIX
Paper from
responsible sources
FSC® C005010

"For the strength of the wolf is the pack and the strength of the pack is the wolf."

—Rudyard Kipling

Contents

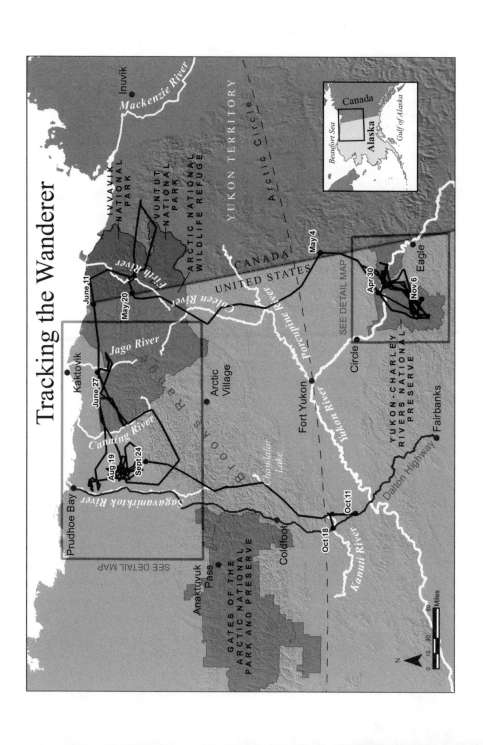

Tracking the Wanderer

Prologue

Where Rivers Meet: Yukon-Charley Rivers National Preserve

On the northern frontier of Canada and Alaska sprawls a wilderness largely devoid of human imprint. Here, the great Yukon River gouges through the bluffs and mountains of an ancient landscape to unmask pre-Cambrian rocks, whose stories reach back eons to the origins of life on earth. Palisades of cliffs, chiseled out by the erosive power of surging water, constrict and bend the Yukon into wide oxbows. Crystalline tributaries— the Charley, Kandik, Nation, and others—tumble from the surrounding highlands and pass through a mosaic of forest, tundra, and muskeg to join the silt-laden Yukon. Gold rush–era mining, trapping, and Native camps and cabins crumble into the soil of dark woods even as willow and alder growth reclaim human trails of bygone days.

The mountain ramparts that scribe the horizons are rolling and gentle, unscathed by the glaciation that hewed other younger but taller subarctic ranges. Just east of the Kandik River, the south-facing slope of Kathul Mountain supports arctic-steppe plants characteristic of the treeless vegetation present across the north during the last ice age. The ancient, dry, cold steppe was rich with grasses, sedges, and sages that supported a mix of large mammals, including wooly mammoths, rhinos, bison, lions, muskox, bears, and wolves. Descendants of some of those animals still thrive here today.

This is a land of extremes. In summer, the temperature soars, with frequent thunderstorms that trigger lightning-sparked wildfires, some of immense size. One fire burned 1.7 million acres, part of a record-breaking Alaska fire season in 2004 that consumed 6.6 million acres, nearly 10,500 square miles. Only the onset of winter truly doused the flames. Winter comes early, sometimes in October, and brings darkness, snow, and killing temperatures. The record low in Eagle City, on the Yukon, is -71°F; the record high, 91°F. Twelve inches of precipitation fall annually, producing about sixty inches of snow. On the winter solstice, there are fewer than four hours of daylight; on the summer solstice, daylight, at twenty-two hours, is almost perpetual.

The patchwork of forest and tundra, mountain and river, supports a convocation of northern wildlife in a setting little changed from a time when only small families of Indigenous people survived here. Each fall, when the hills and margins of the rivers turn gold and the cries of migrating waterfowl fill the sky, today's Han Gwich'in, children of the first people, hunt for moose and caribou to fill their winter larders in the place now called Yukon-Charley.

IN 1980, THE ALASKA NATIONAL Interest Lands Conservation Act (ANILCA) set aside 157 million acres in Alaska as federally protected national parks, national wildlife refuges, national monuments, national forests, wild and scenic rivers, and recreation and conservation areas. New national parks, including Gates of the Arctic, Kobuk Valley, Lake Clark, and others, comprised 43,585,000 acres, more than doubling the country's National Park System. ANILCA was hailed as a triumph by national conservation advocates but widely vilified in Alaska as federal oppression and "the largest illegal land grab in history." President Jimmy Carter was hanged or burned in effigy in several protesting communities, including Eagle, at the edge of one of the new units: Yukon-Charley Rivers National Preserve.

The Yukon-Charley Rivers unit was one of ten national preserves created, some of them contiguous to existing parks. The law called for these new units to be managed much like national parks, except that traditional uses—hunting, fishing, and trapping—would be permitted in recognition of a long history of land use.

Yukon-Charley straddles the highlands between the Tanana and Yukon Rivers on Alaska's border with Canada. The Tanana Hills, taller than the Adirondacks, make up the preserve's rugged spine. Included within the preserve's 2.5 million acres are 115 miles of the Yukon River and the entire Charley River drainage. The area was designed to protect the rivers, its fish and wildlife populations and habitat, and the cultural heritage and subsistence traditions of local people.

The 1,980-mile-long Yukon River is the third-longest river in North America, behind only the Missouri and Mississippi. From its source in British Columbia, the river flows through Yukon Territory in northwestern Canada and westward through Alaska to the Bering Sea, draining nearly 321,500 square miles, an area 25 percent larger than Texas. The name Yukon derives from a Gwich'in Athabascan word meaning "white water river," a reference to the pale color of glacial runoff. During the brief summer season, silt from glaciers turns the river an opaque brown, but in winter the water runs clear beneath ice up to six feet thick.

The 106-mile-long Charley River, a tributary of the Yukon, is one of many streams that tumble from the Tanana Hills, plunging more than three thousand feet before broadening near its confluence with the Yukon. It is the only designated National Wild and Scenic River along the Yukon, with its entire watershed, over a million acres, protected. Some people see it as the most spectacular wild river in Alaska, unsullied and feral.

Yukon-Charley, just fifty miles south of the Arctic Circle, sustains a wide panoply of wildlife adapted to the northern extremes: grizzly bears, Dall sheep, moose, caribou, marten, beavers, otters, foxes, lynx, wolves, and wolverines. Snowshoe hares, also called varying hares for their seasonal color change, cycle from near absence to remarkable profusion, influencing the survival and abundance of lynx, great horned owls, and goshawks—even wolves. Carved river bluffs shelter the highest density of nesting peregrine falcons in North America. In spring, songbirds and shorebirds migrate here from their tropical winter homes to nest and rear their young. Only around a dozen species remain year-round, notably ptarmigan, grouse, owls, jays, and ravens. Each summer, salmon migrate up the Yukon for as much as 1,840 miles to their spawning grounds in the river's headwaters, the longest salmon migration in the world.

Perhaps the most notable, and certainly the most controversial, wildlife species in Yukon-Charley is the gray wolf (*Canis lupus*), a somewhat misleading name, as individuals vary in color from black to nearly white, with intermediate shades of gray and tan. In winter, a wolf's coat is dense and comprised of two different types of fur: a soft, thick underlayer and a coarse outer layer of long guard hairs, with the longest hairs on the back and across the shoulders. Their tails are long and brushy. Wolves have more fur in their ears than dogs to help protect the inner ear from the elements. And like dogs, wolves shed in the spring.

These long-legged, deep-chested wolves are built to run. They have a long, loose stride; flexible wrists; and huge feet, their front feet larger and longer than their hind feet. Wolf tracks are unmistakable, and their width varies depending on the speed of travel. At a gallop or on soft ground, the paw spreads as much as six inches wide and as many long.

Excellent hearing, vision, and acute sense of smell—said to be one hundred times stronger than that of a human—combined with inherent intelligence, make them supreme predators. But wolves do not necessarily possess an inborn tendency to kill, according to veteran wolf researcher L. David Mech, whose seminal work was in the northern-tier states and Canada. Rather, Mech suggests, they are born with certain behavior patterns that allow them to learn to kill. Steps in the learning process include the imitation of the killing behavior of adults and the association of killing with eating.

The rate at which wolves kill large mammals varies with the availability of prey, by season, and with environmental conditions. A pack may take down a caribou or moose every few days during the winter, then fast until their next kill. But hungry wolves will eat almost anything, and in summer they rely on smaller prey to get by. They supplement their diet with squirrels, snowshoe hares, beavers, birds, and fish, particularly spawned-out salmon. When snowshoe hare populations cycle to high levels, wolves feast. Biologists at Denali National Park once observed thirteen wolves chasing a single hare, which somehow escaped. The researchers later found the pack had killed at least four hares in that same covert. In some years the survival of a breeding pair's pups may be linked to hare abundance.

Wolves reach sexual maturity at age two, but they rarely breed until they are three or four. Few wolves live beyond ten. Wolves found in Yukon-Charley are larger and healthier than wolves in more southern regions. Mature males range in size from 85 to 115 pounds. Females are slightly smaller, from 75 to 90 pounds, and seldom more than 110 pounds. Exaggerated stories of enormous wolves float through Alaskan lore. Renowned hunter, trapper, and teller of tales Frank Glaser said that in 1939, he caught a 175-pound male on the Seventymile River, reportedly the largest ever recovered. In 2001, wildlife biologist John Burch of the National Park Service caught a 148-pound wolf just outside the preserve. An accompanying female wolf weighed 110. "They were on a moose kill," Burch recalled. "He had a stomach full of meat and so did she. I would classify any wolf over 140 as huge and extremely rare."

There are an estimated 60,000 to 70,000 wolves in North America, with between 7,700 and 11,200 in Alaska. They range throughout mainland Alaska and many of the islands, with the fewest in the western and northern Alaska coastal zones. The Alexander Archipelago wolf, *Canis lupus ligoni*, found in southeast Alaska, tends to be darker and somewhat smaller than those in central Alaska. Coastal wolves eat Sitka deer but derive much of their diet from the ocean. Some scientists recognize two separate Alaska subspecies, *Canis lupus* and *Canis lupus ligoni*, based on genetic studies, but others tend to lump the two together as *Canis lupus*.

Wolves were called out as a key indicator species in the legislation that established Yukon-Charley. A healthy population of wolves requires a robust, functioning ecosystem, and a faltering apex predator community signals broader concerns. An initial survey conducted in 1985 estimated that forty-nine wolves, divided among nine packs, lived within the boundaries of Yukon-Charley, with a half dozen more from adjacent packs occupying or using areas peripheral to the preserve. Two years later, another survey identified thirteen packs totaling seventy wolves, although none lived exclusively within the preserve's boundaries.

Residents of the region have long believed wolves to be abundant, even overpopulated, in the Tanana Hills, with a detrimental effect on moose and caribou—they believe the area could support many more moose than the official state estimate of eight hundred. In their view, wolves also limit the caribou population. Such opinions are often unfounded, however; until recently, there were no in-depth studies measuring the quantity and quality of the moose browse or caribou forage. In the far north, the quality and availability of winter range, more than any other factor, limits the abundance of these animals. But wolves continue to take the blame when moose and caribou populations decline.

Because the preserve protects the vital calving grounds of a caribou herd highly prized by human hunters and is a popular moose-hunting zone, some wildlife researchers view it as a laboratory where they can explore fundamental questions about predator-prey dynamics. Few places in the north support such an abundance and variety of prey species and their predators. Biologist Bruce Dale, supported by his supervisor Layne Adams, began a research project in 1993 to study the wolves of the preserve. His previous research in Gates of the Arctic National Park showed that prey numbers within wolf territories dropped quite low, but not low enough to show a decrease in kill rate, and the 1993 study shed further light on this key issue. The new study would reveal answers to many questions such as: How many wolves lived there? In how many packs? How big were their territories? What diseases, if any, were present in the population? What did they eat? What was their impact on caribou calving? On moose? On sheep? The study would not only yield information about prey relationships and population dynamics but also highlight the contentious issues arising from the implementation of differing state and federal wildlife management policies.

1

Wolf 258

In early November 2010, two wolves coursed the open slopes above Copper Creek, a tributary of the upper Charley River. Snow from a recent squall persisted in the lee of granite tors, and ice rimmed the shadowed rivulets. Scattered caribou grazed on a nearby ridge, while a nervous band of Dall sheep climbed sheer cliffs. The wolves, alert, were hunting.

The day was sunny and unseasonably warm, at 45°F, and the wind light, ideal conditions for flying. When the wolves heard the helicopter approaching fast and low, they broke into a run. As it grew louder and closer, the wolves parted ways. One, a black female known to biologists as Wolf 227, wore a radio collar. The helicopter was locked onto her signal, betraying her and her companion.

Biologist John Burch signaled to the pilot that he wanted to dart Wolf 227's companion. As the helicopter closed in, the companion wolf veered wildly to shake the pursuit. But the pilot was an expert at chasing wolves. On this tundra hillside, escape was improbable. Sitting in the open door, and blasted by rotor wash, Burch fired his tranquilizer gun and struck the wolf's flank with 500 milligrams of Telazol, a safe, fast-acting veterinary anesthetic that has an analgesic effect. The small helicopter flared and banked away. Within a few minutes, the wolf went down.

Burch, tall and soft-spoken, had been tracking Yukon-Charley wolves since 1996, when he took over the fieldwork from biologist Nick Demma. A Minnesotan, Burch earned a bachelor's degree in wildlife biology from the University of Minnesota and a master's degree in wildlife biology from the University of Alaska, Fairbanks. While still an undergraduate, he began working with L. David Mech in Minnesota on a variety of wolf research projects. Before coming to Alaska in 1985 to conduct wolf research in Denali National Park and Preserve for Mech, Burch worked tracking and trapping wolves for the US Fish and Wildlife Service, primarily in Minnesota and Wisconsin. Burch had more than two decades' experience working with wolves when he joined the Yukon-Charley project. When it came to catching and handling wolves, he had few peers. Over his career, he darted and collared between four hundred and five hundred wolves.

Colleagues regarded Burch highly. "John is one of the most competent field biologists I have ever worked with," said Adams. "At Yukon-Charley, John became recognized as the guy you wanted along if you were working in remote locations. He's one of those adept field folks who can adapt to whatever he is facing, fix anything, work for long stretches under trying environmental conditions, and keep a good attitude throughout it all."

After the helicopter landed, Burch hurried to the sedated wolf. A quick appraisal showed this young wolf was tolerating the drug. Burch had about an hour before it would begin to revive.

The sedated wolf weighed 103 pounds and was about two years old. He was well furred and appeared to be in excellent health, with perfect teeth. Based on their location and previous sightings, he guessed that the young male, now designated Wolf 258, was a disperser from the Seventymile River Pack.

Wolf researchers typically apply sequential numbers to their collared subjects, such as Wolf 227 and Wolf 258. Naming conventions for other wolf projects vary slightly. In Voyageurs National Park, for example, each collared animal is identified with VO, such as Wolf VO77, for Voyageurs. In Denali National Park, wolves get a four-digit code with letters for their color and sex—Wolf 1804GM (GM for gray male) or Wolf 1841GF (GF for gray female). The first two digits represent the year the wolf was collared, and the last two indicate where it falls in the order of wolves collared that year. Common names, such as Blackie or George, are anathema to biologists, who avoid anything anthropomorphic.

After fitting the male wolf with a GPS collar, Burch, assisted by the pilot, collected vital signs: temperature, pulse, respiration rate, and blood oxygen level. They then took cheek swabs and hair samples and drew some blood, both to check for disease and to perform genetic analysis. (Analysis later confirmed that the two wolves were unrelated.) They weighed the wolf and examined his teeth for clues as to its age and condition. Burch finished just as the wolf began to revive. The wolf would be left to recover quietly on his own, although these days, biologists stay with a sedated wolf until it has recovered fully.

The young gray-and-white male was traveling with a collared female Burch knew well. He had first captured Wolf 227, then the breeding female of the Edwards Creek Pack, three years earlier. For the past two years she'd been traveling alone as the last surviving member of her pack, seldom venturing out of her core range on Washington Creek. This capture site on the upper Charley River was out of her normal territory; she had ventured into the range of the Seventymile River Pack, whose territory extended east from the upper Charley River into the Seventymile River drainage. Early in the summer, Burch had spotted her traveling with another wolf and thought she'd paired up. The young male wolf he'd just collared confirmed his suspicions, and he was keen to find out if the sedated male was just a running partner or a mate to Wolf 227. Although two wolves are often called a pack, the key determinant is whether they produce pups.

Dominant wolves breed, fight, and are able to pull down a caribou alone. Researchers typically capture and radio-collar one to three individuals, primarily the breeders, in each wolf pack in a study area. Other pack members hunt and defend territory, but they don't breed or make decisions for the group. Because the breeding pair is least likely to leave a pack, researchers routinely capture and collar them. Burch caught Wolf 227 later that afternoon and replaced her old, failing collar. Despite running solo for two years, the six-year-old female had killed enough prey to stay in superb condition. She'd also managed to hold on to her core territory—or at least avoid lethal contact with trespassing packs. The collars would reveal mating and denning behavior. How the new pairing would affect territorial dynamics was but one of many questions Burch hoped the tracking collars would answer.

At the time, biologists used two types of radio collars to track wolves. A conventional radio collar, in use for decades, transmits a pulsing signal that can be tracked from an aircraft equipped with a receiver and antennae. A GPS collar, on the other hand, transmits coordinates through a satellite to a computer, allowing biologists to more accurately monitor a wolf's travels, life, and death. Like a radio collar, a satellite collar can be tracked from aircraft, but the big difference is that location data is collected automatically. A GPS collar reveals a wolf's day-to-day movements across territory in search of food; thus a wolf remaining close to a particular site for a day or two may indicate it has killed a prey animal and is feeding. Biologists began putting GPS collars on wolves in the Yukon-Charley National Preserve in 2003. Burch was confident that the two new collars would transmit valuable information about the fate of the Edwards Creek Pack, one of a dozen he monitored then. Before flying off, Burch paused for a few moments of silent contemplation. He never seemed to lose his appreciation for wolves and the surrounding wilderness.

WOLVES TYPICALLY HOWL TO FIND one another. A couple of days later, Wolves 227 and 258 reunited about fifteen miles downstream on the east bank of the Charley River. Over the next few days, they wandered into the Seventy-mile River drainage on the far eastern side of the preserve, perhaps a hint at Wolf 258's origin. Then they visited the bank of the ice-rimmed Yukon River, forty miles east, as the raven flies, from the capture site, where the weather turned cold and snowy.

Over the next two weeks, the pair hunted Wolf 227's core territory between Washington Creek and Fisher Creek. The lower portions of the tributaries that drain into the Yukon River are fringed with ideal moose habitat: a forest mosaic of dense timber, and open willow tangles where they can browse in twilight, then hide and rest in cover in midday. Caribou also sometimes graze the open ridges between the two creeks. However, the tracking collars did not indicate that the wolves brought down either.

Heavy snow fell in early December, turning the silt banks, cliffs, and forests white and skimming over the slack waters. Then a cold snap descended; prolonged -40°F temperatures froze the rivers and lakes. On the Yukon, ice fog drifted above open leads and tortured river ice. Near the winter solstice, with less than four hours of daylight, the wolves trotted upstream and passed an exposed, ice-encrusted geologic landmark, the Rock of Ages. Prior to freeze-up, the Yukon is often low and begins to run clear, and this reef of pre-Cambrian rock, deposited nearly five hundred million years ago, before the evolution of shelled fossils, is exposed only at low water. When the wolves trotted past, the river had largely frozen over. The cold made travel easier for the wolves, but foraging more difficult for moose and caribou.

A few days later, on Christmas Eve, the wolves killed a moose three-quarters of a mile upstream from the mouth of the Nation River, a prominent Yukon tributary, and forty-six river miles downstream from Eagle. A half inch of snow fell that day, adding to a two-foot base. The thermometer read -18°F, a slight break from the prolonged cold snap.

Moose are dangerous prey. A big bull weighs ten times more than a wolf and will fight back when attacked, striking out with both antlers and hooves. A single kick from a moose can kill a wolf, or break its jaw, shoulder, or back, resulting in a lingering death. More often than not, wolves fail to bring down the moose they attack. But bull moose enter the winter in relatively poor condition due to the rigors of the rut, or breeding season, which ends in early October, and deep snow and prolonged cold can weaken them further. The data from the collars offered no insight into how the wolves had taken down their prey, only that they'd made a kill. A flyover confirmed it was a moose. Perhaps it had been injured or was debilitated.

The downed moose would last them for days, unless another pack chased them off. Ravens and gray jays pilfered meat from the carcass, and their comings and goings could betray the kill to other scavengers. The kill site was on the edge of the Nation River Pack's territory. Because wolves vigorously defend home ground, even this short incursion into a neighboring territory was perilous, but hunger is a powerful motivator.

When prey is scarce, adult wolves can endure days or even weeks without eating. A wolf can survive on about two and a half pounds of meat per day but requires closer to five to seven pounds per day to reproduce successfully. Near this kill, the pair spent the next two weeks each gorging on as much as twenty-two pounds of meat at a time.

A short distance away, near the Nation's confluence with the Yukon, stands a cabin built in 1934 by trapper Christopher "Phonograph" Nelson, nicknamed for his nonstop chatter. A Norwegian immigrant, Nelson moved to Eagle in the 1920s and developed traplines along the Nation River. Nelson lived in the area for almost thirty years until his death in the cabin in 1949—a river traveler found his frozen body in his bunk. In 1995, the Park Service restored the cabin and designated it for public use. No one was there when the wolves brought down the moose, but trappers would soon work the area again.

IN MID-JANUARY, THE WOLVES LEFT the Nation and trotted back downstream on the Yukon River to the mouth of Washington Creek. Whether they were driven off or had finished with the moose is unknown. In tall timber near the mouth of the creek, they killed again, perhaps a caribou or moose calf, or scavenged carrion. The wolves spent three days lingering between a small frozen lake and the Yukon, well within Wolf 227's core territory. She knew exactly where to find moose browsing in the willows or caribou cratering for lichens on the higher ridges.

The pair next climbed into the highlands just east of 5,620-foot Mount Sorenson, an area frequented by a few Dall sheep and wintering caribou. They appeared to be hunting both species. Persistent winds scoured the alpine forage of snow, building drifts thirty feet deep in the ravines and draws below. The mountain's western face is rugged with minimal forage. The eastern slopes are fairly gentle and rolling with good forage for sheep, but the terrain offers few opportunities to escape, leaving the sheep vulnerable. West of Sorenson, a well-worn sheep trail descends the ridge above Highland Creek to the bluffs above the Charley River. The wolves knew the areas favored by their prey and used the terrain and trails in their hunt. Since these uplands were out of Wolf 227's home territory, her hunting partner likely led the way into familiar terrain.

In the more than two decades that John Burch tracked wolves in the preserve, he documented only eight sheep killed by wolves, a sharp contrast to a wolf study in Denali National Park, where sheep were an important prey species. The GPS collar data indicated that the preserve's wolves spent very little time traveling in sheep country, and Burch speculated that there weren't enough sheep to make hunting them worthwhile. He concluded, contrary to popular opinion, that the wolves had little impact on the sheep in the preserve.

After a few days in the mountains, the wolves returned to their earlier moose kill on the Nation River. Perhaps the memory of abundant meat lured them back, or they expected to find other moose in the same area. Wolves often revisit old kills multiple times, sometimes weeks or even months later, either seeking food or for reasons beyond human ken. But they found only gnawed bones and matted hair. Next, the wolves explored ten miles upriver, risking a foray into the Nation River Pack's territory again, but killed nothing.

By the end of January, they had moved back west to the ridges above the Seventymile River, an area with a long history of mining and trapping. The wolves briefly approached a tractor trail that runs from Eagle to the mining claims but avoided the cabins and work sites. They appeared unusually wary of any human activity.

The bitter cold and darkness tested their hunting skills, strength, and resilience. In withering wind, they again returned to the moose carcass on the Nation. Soon, in early February, in an alder thicket on a steep hillside above the old kill, Wolf 227 foundered and died, just days before breeding season.

By the time John Burch retrieved her GPS collar, a wolverine had scavenged her remains, obliterating any chance of determining the cause of her death, whether an accident, disease, injury inflicted by a moose, conflict with another pack, or any number of causes. Judging by her recent movements and lack of success hunting, Burch believed that she'd grown desperate and starved. If so, she was not the first of her pack to die of starvation. Another related female had suffered a broken jaw, likely from being kicked by a moose. Desperation drove her to kill a porcupine. When she was found, her face, mouth, and throat were filled with deadly quills, some of which had worked their way deeper, puncturing her lungs and heart.

One of Burch's colleagues didn't believe Wolf 227 had starved, because she had been in excellent condition just three months earlier, when recollared, and had been making kills in her territory prior to killing the moose on the Nation River. Nor did he believe that the moose had mortally injured her, because she continued moving around the kill for nearly two weeks afterward and then went on an extended foray into the mountains. Because the kill site was inside the Nation River Pack's territory, he pointed to interpack strife as a more plausible cause of death. If she was not killed by other wolves, he suggested that the female may have been mortally injured during an attack on another moose.

Whatever caused his partner to die, Wolf 258 was now alone.

2

Wildlands, Wildlife, Indigenous People

Northeast Alaska and the adjacent Yukon Territory are lands of legend, made famous by the searing tales of Jack London and Robert Service. In the depths of winter, a harsh, inhospitable terrain gripped in darkness and stabbing cold has long tested human mettle and molded the wildlife that roams the area. Sprawling along the Canadian border north from the Alaska Highway for over four hundred miles to the Beaufort Sea, the region lies in the brutal grasp of winter for up to eight months a year. For long periods, vast swaths of stunted black spruce in the boreal forest are nearly lifeless. Some animals survive underground in deep sleep; others move on. Yukon-Charley National Preserve is but a microcosm of this sprawling wild land and its inhabitants.

The Indigenous Han Gwich'in ("people of the river") have roamed this landscape for thousands of years. Ancestral people traversed the unglaciated Yukon corridor during the ice ages and thrived, despite the subarctic weather, on abundant plants and wildlife.

The forebearers of the modern-day Gwich'in were nomadic, moving wherever game was plentiful. And nowhere was game abundant, winter the limiting factor. On the north side of the Yukon River, in the Ogilvie Mountains, and sometimes down to the river's edge, caribou pulsed through seasonally, sometimes in astonishing numbers, followed by extended periods of complete absence. On the south side of the river, the tundra vegetation of the Tanana Hills' uplands sustained the Fortymile Caribou Herd throughout the winter and during the spring calving season. When the caribou migrated in fall, the Han hunted bulls and cached the meat. Caribou, cached and preserved, could sustain life through the long winter, the skins providing clothing and sleeping robes.

Like other northern caribou, bull caribou in the Tanana Hills weigh 275 to 375 pounds, females about 200 pounds. Bull caribou live about seven to eight years; cows often live ten to fifteen years. Caribou are the only deer in which both sexes have antlers. Large bulls shed theirs in late fall, just after the breeding season, while young males lose theirs later. Pregnant females keep their antlers all winter, shedding them soon after they calve. Females that are not pregnant shed theirs during the winter. Aboriginal hunters sought bulls because of their size and autumn layer of fat, but in lean times they would kill any caribou they could.

The Han Gwich'in, like other Alaska Natives, suffered periodic famine. If the salmon runs failed, or the caribou didn't migrate in the usual pattern, they went hungry. True subsistence is a struggle for survival. Consequently, the Han view of the natural world was complex, with deep spiritual connections. Because their precarious lives were inextricably tied to the land and water, they took care not to offend or insult the provider of life.

Moose live in this wilderness year-round and were, and still are, highly prized by all Gwich'in people. These animals provided not only an abundance of meat but also hides for clothing and shelter. The riverine collage of forest and open muskeg supports a healthy population of Alaska-Yukon moose, the largest deer in the world. Bulls can top 1,300 pounds. With their long legs and neck, dense hair coat, and acute hearing and sense of smell, moose are supremely adapted to life in the far north. In winter, the big deer power through deep snow to browse on the willow and poplar twigs and stems, eating as much as fifty-five pounds per day. In summer, they wade deep into ponds to access sodium-rich aquatic plants. Despite their somewhat ungainly appearance, moose can run up to thirty-five miles per hour and readily swim long distances. The Han stalked them on snowshoes in winter and by canoe in summer. Smoked or dried, the meat was a staple of life for Indigenous people across the north. But they were dangerous for a hunter armed with only a bow or spear. Rifles, once they became available, swung the balance in favor of the hunter.

Hunters focused on moose once the caribou herds had migrated away, or failed to appear at all, but the moose's fortunes, too, hung on the vagaries of winter. They were seldom abundant, and in bad winters, deep snow brought starvation and gave wolves an advantage that few animals could withstand.

The Han occasionally climbed into the peaks to hunt another year-round resident. Dall sheep, the only all-white mountain sheep in the world, are thinly scattered in the Tanana Hills. Summer and winter range is relatively abundant, but the rocky, steep cliffs offer little chance for escape, making the sheep vulnerable to predation. Consequently, a significant portion of the population lives low on the cliffs above the Charley River, where they find haven in the sheer rock. At spring lambing time, in late May or early June, ewes seek solitude and protection from predators in the most rugged terrain available. Lambs weigh less than ten pounds at birth, but adults weigh from 130 to 225 pounds, and their dense winter coats, which can be up to two inches thick with coarse outer hairs over a fine wool coat, often make them look much larger. Rams have distinctive curled horns, while ewes' short, slender horns resemble those of a mountain goat. Because they live in the harsh northern alpine year-round, a sheep that lives twelve years is considered quite old.

Sheep meat is especially palatable, tasting nothing like mutton but more like a fine, delicate venison. Ram horns were coveted and hewn into a variety of utensils. Ice and snow often rendered the sheep hills inaccessible, but the Han hunted them on the Charley River bluffs and sometimes on the cliffs along the Yukon itself.

Some Yukon-Charley sheep are notable for the dark pelage on their back, shoulders, and tail. These sheep are often called Fannin sheep, popularly believed to be an intergrade of the Dall sheep and darker Stone sheep commonly found in Yukon Territory and British Columbia. The Ogilvie Mountains in the northern part of the preserve contain the only known Fannin sheep in the National Park System.

Beginning in late spring, Indigenous people once again shared the land with both black bears and grizzly bears newly emerged from hibernation. Both species wander the forests and riparian zones of Yukon-Charley and hunt moose calves in the shadowy thickets. Higher up, grizzlies seek out the roots of alpine vegetation and hunt newborn caribou calves. Salmon provide a source of protein for both species but not in the abundance enjoyed by coastal bears. Consequently, Yukon-Charley's bears are not oversized, unlike their southern relatives.

By autumn, many grizzlies have left the forest to forage in the uplands for blueberries and crowberries. Their smaller cousins stick closer to the timber for protection, as a black bear far from the tree line is vulnerable to both wolves and grizzlies. Prior to hibernation, which can last nearly seven months, both bear species gorge on whatever they can find, particularly blueberries and soapberries, to bulk up. Even today, a fat bear is a prized addition to a subsistence hunter's larder, but hunting them armed with only primitive weapons was risky. Because they hibernate for many months, bears are available for only part of the year. In late winter, a few Gwich'in hunters were adept at locating breathing holes in the snow above the lethargic black bears' dens and killing them, the fresh meat sometimes the difference between life and death.

Although bears are largely inactive for half the year, their presence inspires outsized wariness in other wildlife and humans alike. Even to this day, some Athabascan people, like their forebears, do not speak of bears, wolverines, or wolves directly because they do not want to provoke their spirits. Whenever a hunter killed a wolf, he put fish or meat in its mouth as a final offering to appease the spirit.

The Gwich'in shared the land with wolves, though perhaps uneasily. Wolves competed with them for food. Their paths crossed in the wake of the caribou herds, at animals slain by people, or near human meat poles or caches. Gwich'in hunters sometimes took meat from fresh wolf kills; wolves sometimes repaid the favor. Interior Alaska Athabascans speak of people gone missing, presumably killed by wolves. Verifiable or not, the old stories are not uncommon or easily dismissed.

As needed, the Han removed wolf pups from dens and kept them in captivity for crossbreeding with their pack dogs. (DNA studies suggest that domesticated dogs accompanied the first humans across the Bering land bridge from Asia to America over fifteen thousand years ago.) The Han's dogs were work animals, not pets. They carried supplies and often assisted in the hunt. In the early 1900s, a traveling physician made this observation: "The native dog proves a most useful domestic animal of burden. . . . They are wolfish and snap viciously at any attempt to caress; in fact, they are generally three-fourths to seven-eighths wolf."

Northeast Alaska supports a limited number of large mammals per acre, but periodically small mammals, notably voles, red squirrels, and snowshoe hares, are abundant. When these populations soar, the populations of their predators, like lynx, foxes, marten, and wolves, also increase. The furs of these predators, along with those of beavers and otters, have long clothed and protected the Gwich'in. But vole, red squirrel, and snowshoe hare populations rise and fall, impacting predators and human hunters alike. When in superabundance, hares dramatically impact their browse—even outcompeting moose for the same plants. Scarcity, on the other hand, can last over a decade.

In days gone by, Gwich'in people hunted hares with bows, spears, snares, and even thrown rocks. Hares weigh from three to four pounds, but their meat is exceedingly lean. Folktales tell of some Indigenous people and prospectors starving when restricted to a diet of hare meat. A few hares, though, could assuage hunger until larger game could be procured. Wolves, too, suffer when hare populations crash. Although considered apex predators of large ungulates, they are opportunistic. Snowshoe hares appear to be an important secondary prey species that affects the survival of wolf pups in particular.

LIVING OFF THE LAND in the far north has never been easy, especially over the long, brutal winters. Despite the deep cold, wind, and darkness, using snowshoes, the Han hunted for hares, grouse, ptarmigan, and moose to survive. Given the unpredictable availability of both large and small game, most Interior Athabascans moved to the riverbank in the spring, where they built canoes, ingenious fish wheel traps, and nets to catch the chum and king salmon that helped sustain them through the harsh winter. All summer long, they caught and dried large quantities of fish to be eaten year-round. (They also dried fish to feed their dogs, thus the source of the name "dog salmon" often used for chum salmon.) But for the Han Gwich'in, food gathering, preservation, and storage were of paramount importance in preparation for winter. Native people up and down the Yukon and its tributaries still gather at summer fish camps as they have for generations, since the salmon harvest is a vital part of their culture.

Gwich'in hunters in summer also sought black bear, feasting on the fresh meat and preserving the tallow and hides. They killed moose and caribou in any season, smoking and drying the meat over smudge fires. Hunters sought the ungulates using dogs during the fall rutting season, when they are less wary, the nights cold enough to lightly freeze meat, and the insects less bothersome.

White explorers began filtering up the Yukon in the mid-1800s, when Alaska was still owned by Russia. Most came in search of gold. Gold discoveries on the Fortymile River and elsewhere sparked small stampedes, bringing ever more miners into the country. During the 1896–1903 gold rushes, the Yukon was the principal transportation route for stampeders, who used steamboats in summer and dogsleds in winter. Between Eagle and Circle City in 1900, there were several small towns on the Yukon within the boundaries of the future preserve. Seventymile City, Charley River, Nation City, and others saw their populations fluctuate with every new gold discovery. A huge discovery in 1897 on the Klondike River (the *Tr'ondëk* in the native language) sparked the world's largest gold stampede, bringing thousands of gold seekers to the region and forever altering the Gwich'in way of life. These newcomers, many armed with the latest firearms, competed with Native people for game but often lacked the skills necessary to preserve and store it.

Traders followed the gold seekers. Fur became a currency, and fur trapping became an important way of life for the Gwich'in. The once nomadic people began to settle near trading posts and gold-rush towns, bartering furs for firearms and other coveted items. But in an all-too-familiar pattern, the Han were often cheated, maltreated, or exposed to disease by the newcomers.

Sobered by the long, brutal winter and near starvation, most newcomers departed almost as quickly as they had arrived. Those who remained adopted some of the lifeways of the Gwich'in to survive: hunting, fishing, and gathering. But they also carried with them the Old World view of wolves and bears as malevolent beasts to fear and eradicate.

Grizzlies, aggressive and powerful, awed many of the newcomers. While black bears almost always retreated, grizzlies might attack, especially when protecting their cubs or defending meat caches, and they often seemed immune to gunfire. Tales of horrific encounters with grizzlies circulated across the northern gold camps. Eradication was seen as the answer to the "bear menace." No means of killing them was overlooked: poison, set guns, steel traps, and deadfalls.

While bears were widely feared because they were dangerous, wolves were both feared and loathed, primarily because they were viewed as competitors for scarce game. A wolf had no right to a moose or caribou that might feed hapless prospectors. An old Russian adage holds that "If you speak *for* the wolf, speak against him as well." Gold seekers, most of them European immigrants, never spoke for the wolf.

3

The Wolves of Yukon-Charley

Many seasons before Wolf 258 and Wolf 227 teamed up, a gray wolf from the Edwards Creek Pack stood atop a mound of dirt in front of a den, listening to the tantalizing sounds below. He'd heard these sounds a few times before. The scent rising from the cool opening of the burrow, initially excavated and used by red foxes, told him what he needed to know: his mate had given birth, five pups in all. This was not the first litter he'd sired, nor the first borne by his mate, who would be solely responsible early on for the pups' care. To grow, they would need meat, and a lot of it. All five adult wolves in the pack would hunt to bring back food for the insatiable pups and their mother. The litter's survival depended on the hunting success of the pack, as led by the breeding male.

May brought mixed weather to the den hidden in the birches on a knoll near frozen Edwards Creek. One day it would be cold and blustery, with scattered snow driven by the wind; the next calm, with the sun high overhead, the temperature above freezing, and the warmth welcome after the winter. Now the air was still. The azure sky was cloudless, and a bright glare glanced off the white expanse.

The wolf's head rocked back and forth as he listened to the mewling below. Once, he extended his head and neck into the burrow, but a warning growl backed him off. For days to come, the mother would not tolerate another wolf near her pups.

Another sound, a distant drone, diverted the wolf's attention and roused the other three wolves that had been lolling nearby. As the noise grew louder, the four wolves looked up to track the small plane flying toward them. One of the wolves, an older female, darted down to the creek bottom to hide in the sheltering willows. Most wolves fail to react to aircraft sounds, but this one had learned that the clatter in the air meant danger. Over the years she'd seen her pack flourish or falter following the passage of aircraft. Two of the pack had been chased down by helicopters, sedated, and collared by biologists. The mother wolf wore one of the devices. On another occasion, an airplane had pursued and scattered the pack. Two members were killed by shotgun blasts.

The wolves watched as the low-flying plane circled a few times, then moved on. It would be some time before the older female returned to the sun-warmed earth near the den. Though their territory was fully within the Yukon-Charley Rivers National Preserve, the wolves were not entirely protected. Eventually, the mother wolf would become the last member of her pack.

ALL OF YUKON-CHARLEY RIVERS National Preserve is wolf country. Typically, ten to twelve wolf packs use some portion of the preserve. While the bulk of some territories lies fully within its boundaries, because of Yukon-Charley's size and shape and the distribution of prey, packs cannot survive exclusively within it. Local densities of ungulate prey determine a pack's home range, and those ranges further shape the resident wolves' movements. Their survival requires the freedom to roam great distances.

The Edwards Creek Pack (Wolf 227's pack) was one of the packs tracked by biologists in the Yukon-Charley wolf study. They inhabited the heart of Yukon-Charley between Woodchopper and Washington Creeks, covering an area of over one thousand square miles on both sides of the Yukon River. The pack preyed predominantly on moose and occasionally on caribou. Wolves learn by experience to do what yields the greatest reward. Once they've learned how and where to get their next meal, they develop hunting patterns to specialize in specific kinds of prey. When they hunt, they revisit favored sites and old kills, which often brings them into contact with new prey.

Biologists tracked the Edwards Creek Pack from the spring of 1995 through the spring of 1998. During those years the pack ranged in size from five to twelve wolves, averaging seven per year. After a two-year break, the pack was again tracked for another decade, from spring 2001 to spring 2011, during which time it ranged in size from one to six wolves, with an average annual size of three. The pack's first den was dubbed the Twin Ponds Den, based on its location. A few years later the pack relocated to another den closer to the mouth of Edwards Creek.

Biologists often apply common descriptive names and GPS coordinates to den sites. Some pregnant females use the same den year after year, while others select a different den each year. No one knows exactly why, but wolves are individuals, and their behaviors vary, often to the extreme. In the Denali Park study, the breeder in the McLeod Pack seemed to hunt and travel as usual right up until she gave birth, wherever she happened to be—under a tree, in deadfall, or wherever. Then in a week or two she moved the pups to the closest available den. She did this multiple times. Conversely, the female of the Edwards Creek Pack likely chose a new site for no discernible reason, her move having no effect on the pack's home range.

The first wolf captured in the pack, a female, was the only one captured in the project via a live snare instead of a dart from a helicopter. The wolf was snared in March 1995, at a moose kill on the Yukon River, upstream from Coal Creek. While out flying a few days earlier, biologist Nick Demma and pilot Sandy Hamilton had spotted a wolf-killed moose near Coal Creek and landed to set snares, eventually capturing the female.

Over the years, researchers collared seventeen wolves from the Edwards Creek Pack, customarily just the current breeding pair. As with other packs, the collaring revealed valuable insights into the lives, and deaths, of free-roaming wolves. Of the seventeen, four were trapped; four others starved; two were killed by other wolves; one was killed by a moose; another essentially killed by a porcupine; and five others dispersed, their fates unknown. One disperser, Wolf 201, a female, paired with a dispersing male from the Hanna Pack, Wolf 205, and together they formed the Lower Charley River Pack. (Two years later, Wolf 205 was killed by other wolves.) Elsewhere, the Edwards Creek Pack accepted a young female, Wolf 171, a disperser from the Fisher Creek Pack— fairly unusual for a new pack. Eventually, the Edwards Creek Pack withered and all but disappeared, leaving Wolf 227 as the sole survivor until her death in 2011.

BY 2014, BIOLOGISTS IN THE Yukon-Charley wolf study had collared 165 different wolves from a number of different packs, some of which were renamed as the population fluctuated and their territories changed. The fluctuations demonstrated by the Edwards Creek Pack are fairly typical of far-northern wolf packs. Pack members come and go, die or wander, and sometimes other wolves join. Pup production and survival are key to pack health.

The average pack in Yukon-Charley is made up of four to seven wolves, including pups, yearlings, and other adults. Pack size is determined by the type and abundance of prey, as well as other factors such as the season. (Packs are largest in spring after pupping and smallest in late winter right before the pups are born in early May.) Due to limited prey, wolf packs in the high Arctic are often significantly smaller than packs to the east and south. Super packs as large as thirty wolves have been reported from varied habitats in Alaska. In the autumn of 1990, Denali's East Fork Pack peaked at twenty-nine. The Seventymile River Pack in Yukon-Charley topped out at twenty-four wolves. Like other large packs, the Seventymile Pack included two or three litters of pups from more than one female.

The Yukon-Charley wolf study documented not only the population dynamics but the power of a pack: a group of wolves hunting together can bring down large, dangerous prey, such as moose, that a lone wolf could never handle. The pack also has the strength and coordination to defend its territory from encroaching wolves and the den and pups from bears and other predators.

Wolves are highly social animals that live in extended families. The social order in the pack is characterized by a separate dominance hierarchy among females and males. The dominant male and female, sometimes referred to as the "alphas," are the breeders. Their intense bond unites and controls the pack's dynamics. Each pack has only one reproductive pair at a time, with some exceptions. Subordinate wolves who transgress are met with bared fangs and threats.

Wolves spend the entire year determining where food is most abundant and marking and establishing their territory. They locate their dens in the center of that territory to protect the pups from other wolves and minimize conflict between packs. The dens vary in structure. Some feature an elaborate set of holes dug into the ground, often usurped from foxes. Some dens may be located under a tree stump or a downed timber or in a rock cave or crevice. In a few instances, a shallow pit or earthen nest functions as a makeshift den. All offer at least some degree of shelter for the litter. Wolf pups can endure very cold temperatures no matter the type of den, but more elaborate dens protect them from extreme weather, as well as predators. In Yukon-Charley, most dens are located at lower elevations, on dry and snow-free slopes that are open to solar heating and near both water and prey.

Breeding usually takes place in late February or March, and the one-pound wolf pups are born in early May, after a sixty-three-day gestation. The pups are born blind and deaf, unable to open their eyes for two weeks, at which time they begin to take their first steps. Litters average five to six pups in Yukon-Charley but can range from one to a dozen. A litter in the high Arctic averages four, ranging from one to ten. (Litter sizes are difficult to determine. Biologists usually count pups in late August when the entire pack is together and hunting, but this data indicates survival rates when they are counted, not overall litter size. Some may have died in the den or in early summer. Pup mortality varies by year but is high, around 50 percent, primarily due to starvation, injury, exposure, and predation.)

During denning season, in May and June, the resident pack centers its activities around the den but travels widely in search of food, which they carry back to the den to feed the mother and her litter; the pups' survival is tied to the health of the mother and the pack's hunting success. Pups require an estimated three times as much protein per pound as adults do, and prey may be scarce. At about three weeks, the pups may make their initial foray outside the den, but they stay at the den until they wean at about eight weeks. Pups grow rapidly; at ten months, they are already adult size and participating in the hunt.

Wolf packs tend to remain within an exclusive territory, the central core of their home range, which they defend from other wolves. The larger outer area overlaps with adjacent packs' territories. The average size of a wolf pack territory in the preserve is about 1,274 square miles. Over time, packs and their territories fluctuate. Some historic packs in Yukon-Charley have disappeared entirely, with their old home ranges, and even dens, usurped by two or more newly formed pairs. Other home ranges have shifted geographically.

New packs are primarily created when unrelated wolves pair up. Some wolves of both sexes disperse from their natal territories by the age of three. Most wolves have to leave their pack if they want to find a mate and produce pups. The biological imperative to mate and establish a personal territory drives a young wolf to leave the relative safety of an established pack. Biologists estimate that lone wolves comprise 15 to 20 percent of any wolf population. Most wolves that form packs will have spent time alone.

In fact, very few wolves end up as breeders and therefore dominant wolves without first having been lone wolves.

Once paired, dispersers try to establish their own territory in a region with sufficient prey to sustain them. Some of these areas already support wolves but in numbers low enough that deadly conflict is minimized. Dispersers can sometimes work their way into an existing pack, but researchers do not yet know how this uncommon occurrence happens. Researchers have reported pack adoptions in regions where rates of wolf hunting and trapping are high and where disrupted packs may be more likely to adopt, or accept, dispersers into a new social structure. Usually a pack will accept a newcomer as a breeding, or dominant, wolf after the loss of its breeder. A wolf melding into a pack as a subordinate member is rare and has been documented only once in Denali National Park.

Dispersal also prevents inbreeding and increases genetic diversity because a disperser eventually finds and mates with an unrelated wolf. It is not only the primary force for genetic mixing and outbreeding but also a way to repopulate vacant territories, a major factor in wolf dynamics.

Dispersal is a risky business. Without the shared hunting prowess and experience of the pack, a lone wolf might starve, get injured by large prey that they attack alone, or die through other accidents. And by pushing into unknown terrain, a wolf is also more vulnerable to hunters and trappers. The principal cause of wolf mortality, though, is intraspecific strife, and many are killed by other wolves defending their territories.

Dispersers often don't move that far from home. In the Denali National Park study, the average distance was just over eighty miles for females and males alike. About half traveled fewer than forty-five miles before settling down by forming a new pack or joining an existing pack. But longer movements are not uncommon. In 2012, a Denali wolf dispersed almost 400 air miles northwest to the Seward Peninsula on the Bering Sea coast. That same year, in Yukon-Charley Rivers National Preserve, a wolf left the Nation Pack, traveled 844 miles in just three months, and was accepted into a new pack near Nulato, 438 air miles west of his natal territory. The next year, a four-year-old male wolf, a member of Denali's East Fork Pack, turned up in Yukon-Charley, after traveling 200 air miles, and established his own pack in the vacated home range of the Seventymile Pack. An analysis of the DNA extracted from 140 individual wolves revealed that Yukon-Charley Rivers and Denali Park wolves are more closely related to one another than to other populations.

Wolves are not the only northern predators to undertake remarkable journeys. In 2019, a tagged juvenile female arctic fox journeyed from Svalbard, Norway, to Ellesmere Island, Canada, in just over four months, covering 2,700 miles. This five-pound fox averaged about thirty miles a day. Her GPS collar logged one remarkable day when she covered ninety-six miles.

Even relatively sedentary predators can move long distances. A Canada lynx, tagged at Kluane Lake in the Yukon Territory, ended up on the Porcupine River in Alaska, 450 miles to the northwest. One collared Alaskan lynx traveled a thousand miles to the east into Canada's Northwest Territories and was still going at the time of writing. Food shortages appeared to trigger these lynx and fox forays. In winter, hunger can set northern animals wandering or compel them to dine on unexpected fare. Many boreal herbivores will eat some meat when push comes to shove. Snowshoe hares will scavenge other hare carcasses, as well as dead birds, perhaps a critical supplement to their diet in subzero temperatures. In an ironic twist, a trail camera in Yukon Territory captured a snowshoe hare feeding on a lynx, its primary predator. Arctic ground squirrels have been seen hunting lemmings, excavating them from burrows. These discoveries blur the line between herbivore and carnivore and highlight how extremely challenging it is to survive in the far north.

A wolf pack tends to grow to a size its prey will support—when wolf numbers are not controlled by people, that is. When a pack reaches this limit, dispersal becomes a natural way for it to adjust to the food supply. In winters with low snowfall, when caribou and moose tend to be less vulnerable to wolves, the scarcity of prey can trigger wolves to disperse. For a young wolf, there's no benefit to staying with the pack when there isn't enough to eat. In the wake of such winters, packs suffer an increase in natural mortality, fewer pups are born, and even fewer survive.

The death of its breeding adults increases the probability that a pack will disband. Young wolves predictably disperse when the breeding pair, and their centralizing behaviors, such as pup rearing, disappear. Although dispersal has always been an important element of wolf population dynamics, another significant factor may have played a part in the dispersal of wolves from Yukon-Charley packs. Under intense hunting pressure, the region's wolves were killed in large numbers, and entire packs were even eliminated. As part of its charter to protect traditional lifeways, Yukon-Charley Rivers National Preserve allows hunting and trapping within its boundaries. What was occurring around its perimeter, however, was something entirely different.

4

State-Sponsored
Predator Control

The Territory of Alaska, and then the young State of Alaska, enjoyed a reputation as a "sportsman's paradise." Huge moose, vast herds of caribou, and giant bears enticed hunters from around the world. For residents, caribou and moose, prized for their palatable meat, were accessible from the limited road system. Hunting success rates were high. Beginning in the late 1960s, though, and accelerating into the 1980s, the northern paradise lost its luster. More and more hunters were returning empty-handed. Hunters overlooked factors such as a human population that had doubled since statehood, which vastly increased hunting pressure, and the transfer of millions of acres of once-public land to private ownership by Native corporations and parks, refuges, and preserves, which reduced the available hunting areas. Instead, wolves, as always, got the blame.

To increase game herds, the federal government had long waged war on Alaska predators via the use of poisons, including cyanide and strychnine, and other lethal means. The widespread use of poison killed everything that sampled the treated meat, from chickadees to grizzly bears.

Territorial Governor Thomas W. Riggs Jr. called for outright elimination of what he called the "bear menace." He saw bears as an impediment to development. The first federally organized predator control efforts began in 1927 to eradicate bears and ramped up over the years to target additional predators—everything from bald eagles to wolves. Bounties were offered for meat eaters of all stripes, even Dolly Varden trout because they ate salmon eggs. Aerial gunning of wolves by federal agents and the public reduced their populations across much of central and northern Alaska. One Talkeetna-based pilot had four 12-gauge shotguns mounted two on each wing that he could fire from inside the cockpit like a World War II fighter ace. Wolves were not even safe in the national parks: limited but controversial control was conducted within the boundaries of what was then known as Mount McKinley National Park. In 1959, with wildlife management now under state control, poisons were banned, and soon wolves were reclassified from "vermin" to big game and furbearers with seasons, bag limits, and licensing requirements. Bounties were phased out, and payments ended in 1972.

But state-sponsored control didn't end there. The state's relatively low-level efforts, compared to the federal campaign, largely escaped national notice until 1992, when the Alaska Board of Game approved a plan to kill half the wolf population, about three hundred, in a region south of Fairbanks, and to cull them over the next few years in order to boost moose numbers. The program targeted less than 4 percent of Alaska's land area and involved 5 to 7 percent of the state's nonendangered wolf population. Publicity surrounding the plan elicited a national outcry.

Wolf control has long sparked intense controversy and been opposed by conservation groups, as well as many wildlife scientists. Deep emotion drives many protestors. Opponents of control argue that wolves are a natural part of vibrant, self-regulating ecosystems, a check on ungulate populations that would otherwise expand beyond a sustainable level, then crash as the habitat suffered. In their view, these predators help keep prey populations healthy by removing the weak and infirm. (The reality is not that simple. Wolves prey heavily on spring calves and kill healthy adult prey

44

disadvantaged by weather conditions.) Opponents also believe that aerial shooting is unethical and immoral and tarnishes the image of the state and hunting in general. For others, the real issue seems to be whether it is moral and ethical to manipulate one species to increase another. One ecologist long ago described wolves as a key indicator species "because a land that can produce a wolf is a healthy, robust, and perfect land."

Proponents counter that wolves take (some say "waste") the game animals on which Alaskans depend and pose a threat to human safety. Controlling them is common sense. Otherwise, wolves would multiply and reduce herds to next to nothing, holding them down in a so-called predator pit. Instead, control benefits both prey and wolves. The more moose and caribou, the more food for wolves, thus more wolves. Many see the way these predators kill their prey as cruel. The final argument: people, and their needs, come first.

Neither side can be swayed by rational arguments. Opponents are often urbanites influenced by countless pretty pictures of wolves published in books and calendars, usually of undisclosed captive animals. Animal lovers also like wolves because they are strikingly dog-like. Opponents respond to the argument that wolves will "wipe out" the game by asking how that could be possible if all of these animal populations have evolved together for millennia. Proponents, on the other hand, are usually hunters unduly influenced by the stories they read in hunting books and magazines, many of which are driven by politics instead of sound science. Facts mean little. Clearly, what we think we know about wolves is a product of our emotions, biases, and attitudes.

In 1994, then Governor Tony Knowles halted the controversial state wolf control program south of Fairbanks and said he would not reinstate any predator control program unless it was based on solid science, made economic sense, and had broad public support. He then asked the National Academy of Sciences to undertake a scientific and economic review of both wolf and bear management in Alaska. The academy's subsequent report was fair and objective, citing clear evidence that wolves and bears can, under certain conditions, keep moose and caribou populations suppressed for many years, but it found fault with the state's efforts. The report recommended that the censusing of these populations be more rigorous and accurate and that the state conduct enhanced habitat management and studies prior to implementing any control program. It suggested that wildlife policy makers in Alaska need to be more sensitive to signs of overharvesting and more conservative in setting hunting regulations—particularly with moose, caribou, and bears—and in designing the control programs. The review also called for better coordination among the state and federal agencies with jurisdiction over wildlife and wildlife habitats.

Legislators and subsequent state administrations ignored many of the academy's findings and recommendations, mostly to curry favor with certain voters, and pushed ahead with plans for predator control. In fact, to prevent future attempts to stifle such control measures, the Alaska State Legislature passed a unique "Intensive Management Law" that required the Alaska Department of Fish and Game (ADF&G) to kill predators to increase game for hunters—a sharp contrast to the National Park Service's policy to maintain healthy and largely undisturbed ecosystems. The law was instituted in 1994—the same year the academy's report came out and a year after Yukon-Charley's wolf study began—and authorized state employees and private contractors to shoot wolves from aircraft.

The law was based on an interpretation of a clause in the Alaska Constitution that stated that wildlife was to be managed on a "maximum sustained yield" basis for the benefit of the people—which meant, in this interpretation, controlling predators. Some biologists privately argued that the Intensive Management Law would eventually end up stressing habitat and nearly guarantee perpetual boom and bust cycles of ungulates and subsequent predator control. A few others saw maximum sustained yield as an unattainable goal.

Over time, the Alaska Board of Game, a group appointed by the governor that oversees all hunting and trapping in Alaska, further liberalized restrictions on hunting wolves and bears. In some areas, the bag limit for grizzly bears increased from one to two per year. Baiting was legalized for both grizzly and black bears. Black bear sows and their cubs, formerly protected, could be shot in dens using artificial lights. As incentives to increase the kill, the sale of grizzly bear skulls, hides, and claws was permitted. Wolf and coyote pups also could be killed during denning season. Rule changes allowed the use of snow machines to chase down and kill wolves and wolverines. All of these practices—previously illegal and considered unethical, contradicting the principles of "fair chase" hunting—were permitted in an attempt to reduce predation on meat animals and, thus, increase their availability to hunters.

The Intensive Management Law almost immediately put the missions of the State of Alaska and the National Park Service at odds. The ADF&G included the Yukon-Charley Rivers National Preserve within its Upper Yukon–Tanana Predation Control Area (an area of about 18,750 square miles) in an effort to reduce wolves to primarily benefit the Fortymile Caribou Herd, which calved in the preserve, even though the preserve's purpose was to maintain natural processes and wildlife abundance, diversity, and behavior—not reduce one species for the benefit of another.

The status of the Fortymile Herd had long been a contentious issue. In the 1920s, a pioneer biologist estimated it at more than 500,000, which he derived by counting caribou crossing the newly built Steese Highway north of Fairbanks. He estimated that about 1,500 caribou crossed a one-mile section of the road each day continuously for eight days, and further extrapolated that many caribou were crossing at the same rate along a forty-mile stretch of road. Combining those assumptions with some other dubious calculations resulted in his final tally: 528,000. Because early biologists worked without the modern tools of aircraft, photo censusing, and computer models, the counts they came up with were often fanciful. Some contemporary biologists agree there were nowhere near 500,000 caribou, and probably far fewer than 200,000, but clearly no one knows the historic size.

When the herd declined to a low of six thousand in 1974, hunters again blamed wolves. Some biologists disagreed, saying that the actual cause of this crash was unknown; their suspicions included overharvest, food limitations due to range depletion and fires, or other natural factors. In their view, predation was not considered a causal event. But the hunting public demanded action to restore the herd, pushing for expanded control of wolves across the herd's range.

In an ironic twist, some research indicates that intensive predator control fragments packs, which may trigger increased dispersal and reproduction, as well as changes in hunting behavior. The loss of one or both breeding adults may allow subordinate members to breed, resulting in higher pup production, thus initiating another round of control.

Beginning in 1997, state biologists proposed a nonlethal means of wolf control in the Upper Yukon–Tanana Predation Control Area by sterilizing the breeding pairs of designated packs and moving nonbreeding wolves out of the area. (Ultimately fifteen packs were "treated.") Six packs within Yukon-Charley at that time were at risk of control activities because they periodically traveled outside the preserve's boundaries, and the National Park Service requested that these wolves be off-limits. State biologists initially agreed not to treat those that denned in the preserve but asked that the Park Service continue to identify and monitor these particular packs. In their view, the wolves of Yukon-Charley could serve as a valuable control group to compare and contrast to the treated population and those that were sterilized and moved. But critics scoffed at the nonlethal methods, saying the state was "giving in to the tree huggers."

The control program called for a substantial reduction of wolves but ultimately evolved in 2005 to favor lethal means. Beginning in 2006, the area subjected to aerial hunting was greatly expanded to surround the entire preserve south of the Yukon River. Nearly seventy private pilots eventually joined state biologists in the effort and at times did the bulk of the killing. A private sportsman's group in Fairbanks offered cash payments for any wolf killed on calving grounds. Then Governor Sarah Palin's office increased the number to be killed and announced that volunteers would be paid $150 for each wolf. Critics called it a de facto bounty. (The only previous incentive was the value of a pelt, from $200 to $300). Private pilots complained that fuel prices were high and wanted the state to subsidize those expenses too. One participant said he and his cohort needed no incentives as they were "performing a public service." The state billed the predator control work as the "Fortymile Herd recovery effort." State and federal cooperation deteriorated.

Despite opposition, under the Palin administration the state continued to push ahead with plans to increase the wolf kill in the region around the preserve, aiming to boost the survival of caribou calves and allow the herd to expand. In 2009, helicopters were deployed throughout the Upper Yukon–Tanana Predation Control Area, excluding Yukon-Charley, and eighty-four wolves were shot. Others were killed via airplanes and by ground hunters and trappers, for a total of 220 killed that year within the control area.

As neighboring packs were eliminated by these efforts, resident wolves in Yukon-Charley began to regularly sortie outside the preserve's boundaries, which increased their vulnerability. The Yukon-Charley study had been designed to gather information so that managers could make informed, science-based decisions regarding wolves and wolf management in the preserve, but the expanding control effort threatened that objective.

Over a ten-year period, Yukon-Charley lost ninety wolves in all from nine radio-collared packs monitored by the Park Service. A partial tally: in 2005, six wolves from the Threefinger Pack were shot, two of which wore radio collars; nine from the Cottonwood Pack were shot, two of them collared. In 2010, four from the Webber Creek Pack, two collared, were killed, eliminating the entire pack.

Larger packs were eradicated in subsequent years: in the winter of 2012–13, gunners killed all twenty-four from the Seventymile Pack. The next year, they wiped out the entire Lost Creek Pack, eleven in all, two of them collared. The population in Yukon-Charley dropped from eighty-one wolves to twenty-nine, in nine packs—a decline of 64 percent, the largest recorded drop in twenty years. That spring the average pack size fell to 3.2 wolves, the second lowest ever recorded. In 2015, twelve out of thirteen in the Sheep Bluff Pack were shot from a helicopter. This organized wolf kill was unmatched since territorial days when they were killed by federal hunters.

IN 2014, HOWEVER, THE PARK SERVICE paused its twenty-two-year-long study of Yukon-Charley wolves. The decision was made for several reasons, including a lack of adequate funding. In addition, the State of Alaska did not renew the Park Service's permit to collar wolves on state land adjacent to the preserve and refused to stop killing collared wolves outside its boundaries. In fact, by 2016, so many had been killed that aerial hunters couldn't find enough to meet the state's goal.

Meanwhile, the Fortymile Herd had grown to around fifty thousand. Proponents of intensive management pointed to the increase as validation of the control effort. But some state biologists believed factors besides reduced predation on calving grounds were at work; caribou populations naturally experience oscillations, they said. Ongoing research revealed some troubling trends.

Even as the herd grew, the state's own data revealed that calf survival did not increase from 2010 to 2015. Nutrition is vital to adult survival as well as calf production. Herd movements suggested that the range was being overused. Further studies were needed to assess the impact of the herd on its forage and whether its range could provide it with sufficient nutrition.

Beginning in the fall of 2013, the Fortymile Herd ventured farther into Yukon Territory, reaching areas along the Dempster Highway northeast of Dawson City, a region not previously documented within the herd's historic range, and to the southeast across the White River northeast of Beaver Creek. In addition, it continued expanding to the west, into Alaska's White Mountains. Much of the habitat in Yukon Territory and that range to the west appears to support abundant lichens and offer better nutrition. Thus, the expansion of range is likely related to forage conditions.

In 2017, a former State of Alaska biologist published a paper concluding that wolf control was not working: growth of the Fortymile Herd was limited by food and nutrition, not predation. He concluded that unless the herd size was reduced, a population crash might ensue.

In spring 2018, predator control programs in the Upper Yukon–Tanana region were suspended for evaluation. The last photo census of the Fortymile Herd in 2017 counted seventy-three thousand animals, well within the state's management goals for recovery. However, the weights of four-month-old calves, a metric used to assess population health, had decreased, continuing a downward trend. Smaller calves indicate stress on the herd, likely from overgrazing. As of 2021, the herd appears to be in decline, and hunting seasons have been liberalized to prevent further habitat damage. (No efforts to enhance habitat have been undertaken, nor have they been recommended in the state plan.)

Wolf control efforts are currently active in four other areas in Alaska, covering approximately 5 percent of the state's land area. (The four units comprise 33,165 square miles, an area larger than South Carolina.) The stated goal is to reduce predation rates by bears and wolves, allowing humans to take more ungulates while also maintaining sustainable populations of predators.

In the year prior to the pause in wolf control, 140 were killed in the upper Tanana Hills. In January 2021, the population in the control area was estimated at 294 and appears to be recovering after nearly two decades of control efforts. With their numbers approaching normal ranges across the region, wolves will once again play a role in regulating the Fortymile Herd.

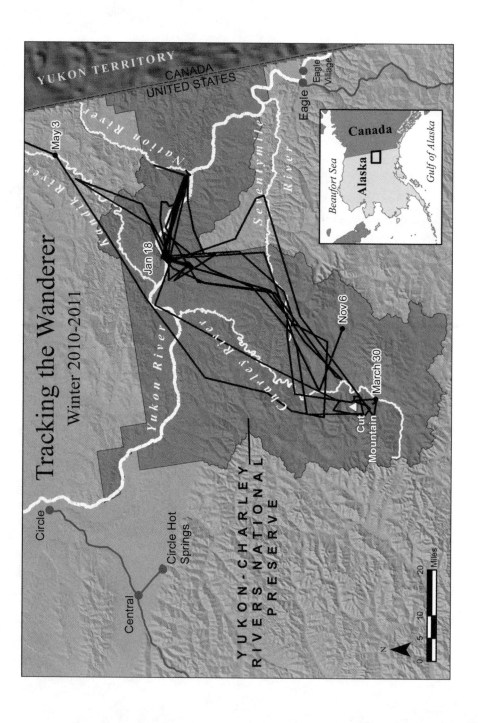

Tracking the Wanderer
Winter 2010-2011

5

The Wanderer

After Wolf 258 lost his partner, he cut back to familiar ground in the highlands above Washington Creek. Twice in late February, he returned to the Nation River, spending the better part of three days apparently searching for his companion and risking possible contact with the Nation River Pack.

Daylight had begun to return ever so slowly in the days after the winter solstice, accelerating as the weeks rolled by. In early March, daylight hours had lengthened to over eleven and a half, gaining nearly seven minutes per day. Though daytime temperatures moderated to near zero, they still fell to -35°F at night. Periods of brilliant sunshine alternated with frequent snow squalls. Patches of rock and bare ground absorbed the sunlight's feeble warmth, uncovering leaf litter and desiccated foliage. In the first days of the month, Wolf 258 reached the upper Charley River, passing near a remote cabin and airstrip built in 1968 by the late Ed Gelvin.

Ed Gelvin arrived in Alaska in 1949 at age twenty-five, a decade before statehood, and headquartered in Central, a small mining village just west of Yukon-Charley. He busied himself as a miner, trapper, hunting guide, and builder of dogsleds and boats. Both he and his son, Stanley, were pilots and miners on prospecting ground that had been worked long before by pioneer gold seekers. The Gelvins lived off of moose and caribou and prospered in self-sufficiency. Ed trapped fox, lynx, and wolverine, as well as wolf, which he hunted from the air. He, like a lot of Alaskans, believed in hunting wolves to control their numbers and limit predation; however, he did not believe in state-sponsored control.

The National Park Service now owns Gelvin's Charley River cabin and tiny airstrip, which it repaired in 2017. Intrepid trekkers and river runners land there at their peril. Few people, if any, visit the area in winter.

During the first half of March, Wolf 258 coursed the slopes and ridges draining Cut Mountain, a location favored by foraging sheep. For a lone wolf, sheep are much easier and safer to bring down than a moose, or even a caribou. The only defense a sheep has is its ability to run from danger and escape into the cliffs and crags. Static GPS locations recorded by the wolf's collar indicated he made at least two or three kills on the ridges above the Charley. He could have brought down either caribou or sheep, but there was no way to know for sure.

In midmonth, he unexpectedly made a fifty-mile jaunt north to the banks of the Yukon, but almost immediately turned around and went right back to where he'd started. On the spring equinox, he again traversed the familiar ridges above Washington Creek. The next day he moved eleven miles northwest to a small island in the still-frozen Yukon, four miles downriver from the mouth of the Kandik River, a clear-water stream birthed in the gray summits of the Ogilvie Mountains. The likelihood of finding prey there was nil. He soon returned to the upper Charley.

From the end of March through the first week of April, Wolf 258 remained at a kill site on a small tributary a dozen miles above Gelvin's cabin, likely feasting on a caribou. With almost fourteen hours of daylight and temperatures rising into the high forties, the snow was melting fast and, for the first time in weeks, open water purled over the cobbles. The weather seemed to fluctuate hourly—sun and warmth one moment, clouds and chill the next. Periodic squalls brought mixed rain and snow.

Three inches of wet snow fell one day, then melted the next under a spring chinook.

For the remainder of April, Wolf 258 roamed familiar terrain, across nearly twelve hundred square miles, from the mouth of Washington Creek to the head of the Seventymile River in the east and back to Cut Mountain in the west, never lingering long in any one place. On April 28, he left the upper Charley and moved fifteen miles north to Coal Creek, a historic gold-mining area. The next night, he moved another twenty miles northwest to the bank of the Yukon, now running heavy with ice, and stopped just across from Biederman Bluff, near the spot he'd visited on the equinox.

The high bluff on the north side of the Yukon was named for pioneer mail carrier Ed Biederman. Beginning in 1912, Biederman contracted to transport the mail down the Yukon River between Circle City and Eagle. He and his Native wife, Bella, built a cabin opposite the mouth of the Kandik. In summer, they ran fish wheels to catch and cure salmon for human use as well as for dog food. In winter, Biederman hauled the mail in a seventeen-foot hickory dogsled, making the 158-mile run from Eagle to Circle in about five or six days. Biederman carried the mail on the Yukon until the mid-1930s, when he lost parts of both feet to a dunking while hauling the mail at -40°F. His sons, Horace and Charles, took over until the service ended in 1938. The Biedermans' dogsled now resides in the National Postal Museum in Washington, DC.

Like a lot of mushers, the Biedermans worked to develop sturdier and hardier dogs suited for the harsh northern climate. Trappers sometimes pulled wolf pups from dens and sold them to mushers to breed with their dogs. These experiments rarely panned out. One musher in that era, Deming Wheeler, made the dubious claim that he ran a full team of wolves. Biederman, like most everyone else, found hybrids to be intractable and aggressive, but he successfully incorporated dogs with limited wolf ancestry into his team.

WOLVES SEEM UNDAUNTED BY vast horizons, unexplored terrain, and distant realms. An eagerness, an incandescent energy, drives them into faraway places, seeking both prey and an intimate knowledge of vital coverts and terrain. A dispersing wolf seeks more than food; it pursues its destiny.

Since his capture and collaring, Wolf 258 had spent nearly six months coursing the very heart of Yukon-Charley Rivers National Preserve, from strands of the Yukon River to the highest summits. He'd endured extreme cold, slicing winds, and long bouts without food. He'd lost his partner but had survived alone. His next move would ultimately determine the course of his life.

Early on the last day of April, Wolf 258 plunged into the ice-choked river and fought for the far bluff, battling the powerful spring flow and dodging nearly a half mile of grinding ice and bergs the size of small cars. Midway in this crossing, he used the eddy at the end of a small island for respite before forging on. Somehow, he reached the far shore uninjured and dragged himself up the shelf ice to the base of the thousand-foot-tall Argillite prominence towering over the river. Later that morning, in sharp sunlight, Wolf 258 stood atop Biederman Bluff looking down at the broad bend of the Yukon. It would be the last time he would see the river and his home territory.

Wolf 258, who we'll now call the Wanderer, quickly negotiated the forested ridges east of Biederman Bluff and dropped down to the Kandik River, where ice still rimmed the river rocks and rotting snow persisted in spruce thickets. Chivying red squirrels marked his movements as he explored every scent, every detail that might lead to food. He paced old moose trails through the maze of forest, brushing against wisps of snagged hair that marked the passage of grizzly bears. He sniffed old squirrel middens, made a run at a spruce grouse cock courting a hen, gnawed old moose bones, and quenched his thirst with ice-cold river water colored with tannin.

The Wanderer kept moving northeast. In the long days and white nights of spring, he passed from the forests of the Kandik River to the alpine tundra above the Grayling Fork of the Black River. Travel was not easy for the hungry wolf, as mushy snow veiled wide swaths of land. Portions of the upper river were still frozen, and other sections pounded with ice and meltwater. Although the first flights of geese had touched down in the lowlands, prey was scarce in the mountains.

At the southern edge of their wintering grounds, the scent of the Porcupine Caribou Herd lay heavy on the land, but few, if any, remained, most having already begun the long march to their calving grounds on the Arctic coastal plain. It would take days of steady travel for the Wanderer to catch up. Gnawing hunger would be his constant companion, eased only by occasional voles, ground squirrels, or scraps of winter kill.

In three days, he had covered seventy-five miles, as the raven flies, from the Yukon River to the foothills of the Ogilvies in Yukon Territory, Canada's westernmost territory. Here, the Dall sheep lambing time was still a month off; it appeared the Wanderer tarried to hunt them only for a day or two before turning back to the northwest and reentering Alaska. Had he continued in the direction he had been going, in a day's travel he would have entered Ni'iinlii Njik (Fishing Branch) Territorial Park, home to moose, grizzly bear, wolf, and mountain sheep. Although he did not know it, he'd have been safer in Yukon Territory; the government had abandoned wolf control efforts there a decade earlier.

YUKON TERRITORY IS LARGELY UNDEVELOPED wilderness, a broad landscape of towering mountains, foaming rivers, tundra, and great tracts of roadless boreal forest. It is the least populated province or territory in Canada; the majority of its thirty-six thousand inhabitants cluster near Whitehorse, the capital. About a quarter of the population is of Indigenous origin, people of the First Nations. Eleven of the fourteen First Nations in Yukon Territory have negotiated and signed comprehensive land claims and self-government agreements with the government of Canada.

Yukon Territory boasts a number of national and territorial parks, some of which have been established through collaboration with the First

Nations. Unique among the parks is Ni'iinlii Njik, a set-aside larger than Delaware. To protect their sacred place, the Vuntut Gwich'in collaborated with the Yukon government to establish the territorial park in 1999. The park and the adjacent Habitat Protection Area preserve the Gwich'in land heritage, as well as a distinct ecosystem. Access by air to the core of the park is tightly controlled.

Ni'iinlii Njik means "the place where salmon spawn." Chum salmon swim almost sixteen hundred miles from the Bering Sea up the Yukon, then the Porcupine River, to spawn in the Fishing Branch River's clear tributary waters. Fishing Branch, although it runs astride the Arctic Circle, never freezes due to the distinctive geologic features that surround it. Groundwater percolates through an intricate system of underground caves, drainage channels, and fissures created by dissolving limestone. In summer, water is naturally stored underground and kept warm, ultimately resurfacing in the river. Salmon runs occur later in autumn here and attract a congregation of feasting grizzly bears. The spawning and spawned-out salmon serve as an abundant source of protein well into winter for meat eaters.

Numerous grizzly bears den in the cavities of Bear Cave Mountain, a site closed to human visitation. The park also protects a portion of the Porcupine Herd's migration route, and moose and sheep live in or pass through the Ni'iinlii Njik. Resident predators stalk the streams, forests, and mountains in search of prey.

WHY DID THE WANDERER TURN away from a land rich with game? How did he choose his direction of travel? Would he pair up soon, or return to home ground? No doubt, hunger played a huge part in his decision-making. Perhaps the lingering scent of caribou altered his course. A hint of prey borne on the wind is better than a multitude of sterile, odorless zephyrs. It's no easy task to find prey that never stops moving, and no matter the direction he turned, he'd have to be cautious, always alert, to avoid intolerant humans and resident wolves. Travel through new country is perilous for a wolf.

Veering back into Alaska on the heels of the migrating caribou, he traveled thirty-nine air miles northwest in one day and paused on the rotting ice of the Salmon Fork of the Black River. Already the gabbling of geese and ducks enlivened the partially thawed waters. The Salmon Fork, which does not thaw until mid-May, meanders across the Yukon Flats, through muskeg, black spruce thickets, and flat land dotted with countless ponds and lakes. It also wends through the territory of at least one resident pack, a small portion of the 150 or so wolves that live there. The Wanderer was trespassing and vulnerable to attack.

The Wanderer now crossed the Arctic Circle for the first time. Rather than being a magic line where one biotic and climatic region ends and another begins, the Arctic Circle relates to the orientation of the earth to the sun, the divide between light and dark, and the place where in summer the sun shines twenty-four hours a day and in winter not at all.

A little farther north, where forest is replaced by tundra vegetation, the tree line is the traditional boundary between the Arctic and sub-Arctic. There's no clear-cut demarcation between forest and tundra; instead the two habitats may intermingle in a zone between fifty and one hundred miles or more wide. Trees thin out as latitude or altitude increases, and their size is limited by the short growing season. In a temperate forest, one eleven-year-old spruce measured three inches in diameter; a boreal forest spruce that same size was eighty-six years old. Also in the Arctic, another ten-inch-diameter white spruce took root in the year 1720. On his present course, the Wanderer would soon leave timber behind to course open, treeless tundra.

The Wanderer was now traversing the wetlands of the Yukon Flats National Wildlife Refuge, the nation's third largest. Like Yukon-Charley, it was created by the 1980 ANILCA legislation. The eleven-thousand-square-mile refuge sprawls between the Brooks Range to the north and the White

Mountains to the south and extends 220 miles along the Arctic Circle from the Trans-Alaska Pipeline corridor in the west to the Canadian border in the east. The weather extremes in this region are remarkable. Alaska's record-high temperature, 100°F, and record-low temperature, -80°F, were set nearby. Myriad bodies of water provide important nesting and rearing habitat for waterfowl from all four North American flyways. Each summer, the refuge supports an estimated two million ducks, the highest breeding densities in Alaska. A varied population of mammals, fish, and birds live in the quilt of muskeg, forest, and riparian habitats.

Just west of the refuge's western boundary is the James W. Dalton Highway, the only road that bisects northern Alaska. The Dalton, or Alaska Highway 11, was built in 1974 as a supply route for the construction of the Trans-Alaska Pipeline and development of the Prudhoe Bay oil fields. The 357-mile road north from the Yukon River cuts near the heart of the least inhabited and largest undeveloped landscape in the United States: the northeast corner of Alaska, the wildest of the wild.

Several hundred Gwich'in live in seven villages in the Yukon Flats area, many of them pursuing a subsistence lifestyle of hunting, trapping, fishing, and berry picking. These communities are accessible only by boat or airplane in summer and snow machines or dogsleds in winter. Numerous cabins and seasonal settlements dot the refuge. Chalkyitsik, which translates as "fish-hooking place," is an important seasonal fishing site, its use dating back to as early as 10,000 BC. Summer-run king and chum salmon swim by the village on their way to spawning grounds upstream. Autumnal chum salmon are traditionally the most abundant species on the Black River drainage.

When the Wanderer crossed the Arctic Circle, he was less than fifty miles east of Chalkyitsik. Village residents were anxious to fish or hunt waterfowl, but with breakup in full swing, few people were on the river. The Yukon Flats are also rich in muskrats, traditionally hunted for their fur shortly after ice-out. Hunters would be about as soon as conditions allowed. For now, the wolf was alone, undisturbed, probably feeding on the thawing salmon remains. Tetthajik Creek, an important spawning stream, flows into the Black River just upstream from where he lingered. The rich protein of those putrid carcasses was irresistible.

Travel during spring breakup is difficult, even for wolves. The snow gives way underfoot and the still-frozen earth pools water on the surface. Thinning ice conceals deeper water, making stream and lake crossings hazardous. A pack travels single file through deep or soft snow, each wolf stepping in the tracks of the one ahead to conserve strength. They also take turns leading to save energy. The Wanderer had no such benefit. He forged north alone, breaking trail across all manner of terrain, river, and snow conditions, stopping often to gnaw balls of snow from between his toe pads. Spots of blood in crusty snow indicated minor abrasions or cuts. He largely traveled during twilight, when the snow briefly firmed up. Despite these difficult conditions, the Wanderer had averaged twenty-five miles per day since leaving the Yukon River.

Continuing north, he heard an unmistakable roar well before he saw the Porcupine River: the river was in midbreakup, with tons of ice ramming downstream at five to eight miles per hour. Typically, it would be solidly frozen over in the first week of May. But this spring, breakup had arrived earlier than normal, the unseasonable warmth triggering rapid snowmelt and flooding. Just a week before, caribou by the hundreds had crossed the Porcupine on solid ice all the way upstream to Old Crow in the Yukon Territory, but in recent days, villagers had seen the animals stranded on floating ice pans; others drowned or were crushed. Crossing now would be difficult and dangerous.

6

Crossing the Porcupine

From the slopes opposite the Porcupine's confluence with the Coleen River, the Wanderer watched the careening ice floes. Already the young wolf had risked his life crossing the Yukon River, and even though the Porcupine wasn't as wide, the ice moved faster, with minimal breaks or open water. Whenever the river jammed, chunks of ice thirty feet high would shoulder up and smash together, crushing anything in between. When the jams broke, the mass would sluice downstream in a rush.

On May 9, the Wanderer charged in to dare the punishing, lethal ice. At times he leaped from pan to pan, plunging into the icy water when forced or knocked down. Somehow, he crossed unscathed. On the north bank, he gave his coat a good shake, pawed the water from his ears, and resumed his journey.

The Porcupine, a tributary of the Yukon, is Alaska's fourth-longest river and one of the major arteries pulsing through the northeast of the state. For millennia, the Gwich'in had used it for transportation and trade, but their traditional way of life was transformed when white fur traders entered the region in the 1800s. Early traders encouraged the Gwich'in to trap and barter furs for goods. Transient newcomers also trapped to support their summer gold prospecting.

To survive the long, bitter winters, fur animals grow thick, rich pelts, the type most prized by the global luxury apparel market. Foxes, marten (sable), beavers, and mink sustained the trade, with foxes once selling for high prices. Itinerant traders scoured the region in search of fur.

Traders came not only to collect furs but also to expand England's influence in the northwest, and they used the Porcupine River to further this mission. In 1847, the Hudson's Bay Company established Fort Yukon at the confluence of the Porcupine and Yukon Rivers, well inside Russian territory. The company's westernmost outpost put it at odds with the Russian-American Company, their powerful trading rival who had their own post at Nulato, downstream on the Yukon. Following the 1867 purchase of Alaska from Russia, American authorities closed Fort Yukon, pushing the company back into Canada. The Hudson's Bay Company relocated upstream on the Porcupine River and built the Rampart House trading post just across the border. An old photo from the early 1900s depicts company factors at Rampart House posing with Gwich'in trappers and bundles of fur, including several large wolf pelts.

But wolves were never a large part of the luxury fur trade. Their pelts are heavy, and their long hair relatively coarse. In the North, most wolf pelts were used for parka ruffs, lap robes, and heavy mitts. While some trappers specialized in catching beaver, foxes, or marten, very few, if any, focused solely on wolves; they are notoriously wary and not easy to trap, shy of anything out of the ordinary. Because people viewed wolves as competitors for meat animals and wanton killers, many were shot or poisoned at every opportunity.

In the early twentieth century, trapping lagged behind only gold mining in the state's economy. Fur production and sales, totaling $4.5 million (about $67 million in today's dollars), peaked in Alaska just before the Great Depression began.

As styles and attitudes changed, prices and trapping pressure oscillated across Alaska and Canada. In the early 1970s, with the dawning of the back to the land movement, a resurgence in rural and wilderness life brought many new people into Bush Alaska. Derelict mining and trapping cabins were rebuilt and old traplines were rejuvenated, especially in the upper Yukon River region. Trapping, both commercial and recreational, waned in the following decades, participation fluctuating in response to fur prices, which tumbled to rock-bottom in 2021.

AFTER CROSSING THE PORCUPINE, the Wanderer traveled north thirty air miles into the foothills framing the Coleen River, a major corridor for migrating caribou. The 186-mile-long Coleen begins in the Brooks Range and flows south fully within the Arctic National Wildlife Refuge, the largest wildlife refuge in the country. Scattered bones, shed antlers, and gnawed caribou racks dot the surrounding tundra, a testament to eons of struggle.

The Coleen tumbles through treeless highlands that in summer are resplendent with wildflowers. Between storms, the crystalline waters rush lyrically over the cobblestones. Once the grade gentles, the river meanders across tundra flats engraved in places with deep, ages-old caribou trails. The tundra gives way to black spruce thickets downstream; mixed stands of tamarack, poplar, and white spruce hem the lower stretches. Logjams, downed timber, and sweepers near the mouth of the river mark its petulant moods. Built-up tiers of ice called *aufeis* persist into July. (Aufeis forms in winter as percolating water along watercourses reaches the surface and freezes, forming ever-thickening layers of ice.) In summer, lupine and fireweed bloom in willow thickets alive with breeding songbirds and ptarmigan. Fields of ankle-twisting tussocks and legions of mosquitoes make travel away from the river toilsome for humans and wildlife alike. In autumn, abundant wild berries feed bears and other creatures.

As he loped north, the Wanderer kept to the hard-frozen tundra to the east, shying from the uncertain waters of the Coleen, where spring runoff pulsed water and ice downstream, its sound a warning to the unwary. On these sun-warmed slopes, plant life stirred from quiescence, the first blush of green mingling with the sere leaves fluttering in the wind.

After two days of hard travel covering fifty air miles, near Dorothy Creek, a west-flowing tributary of the Coleen, the Wanderer caught up with the stragglers of the migrating caribou herd. For the first time in the ten days since leaving the Yukon River, he brought down large prey or found a winterkill. Over the next two days, he feasted and rested in the shadow of the Brooks Range, the Arctic's wild crown.

Named for pioneer geologist Alfred Hulse Brooks, the Brooks Range is the major climactic divide that separates Arctic Alaska from Interior Alaska. The range, born in the Yukon's Barn Mountains eighty miles east of the border, reaches its highest and broadest points in the Arctic National Wildlife Refuge. Rivers on the north side flow into the Arctic Ocean; rivers on the south, like the Coleen, flow into the Yukon River, then the Bering Sea. The Brooks Range contains hundreds of miles of remote canyons, wild rivers, pristine lakes, and a sea of jumbled peaks. It is the last hurdle caribou must cross to reach their calving grounds on the Arctic coast.

After feasting, the Wanderer swam the icy Coleen and trotted twenty-two miles northwest to the divide between the Coleen and Sheenjek Rivers, where scudding clouds tore on the peaks and a persistent wind pushed snow squalls across the valley. The Sheenjek, a designated Wild and Scenic River, figures prominently in the history of America's wilderness preservation movement.

IN 1956, BIOLOGIST OLAUS MURIE and his wife, Margaret, led a two-month-long expedition to the Sheenjek, locating their main camp at Lobo Lake, a place not far from where the Wanderer rested on the divide. Financed by the New York Zoological Society and the Conservation Foundation, the expedition sought to make a detailed and comprehensive natural history study of the region as part of the push for wilderness preservation. The Muries also worked with the Wilderness Society (founded in 1935), which lobbied for and eventually won passage of the Wilderness Act in 1964. Long enthralled with the austere Arctic, the Muries vowed at Lobo Lake to protect America's last remaining patches of wilderness and fight to establish the Arctic National Wildlife Refuge; their long years of dedication paid off in 1960 with its creation. Their time together at the "lake of the wolf" proved to be a pivotal moment in conservation history.

Olaus Murie came to Alaska in 1920 as an assistant biologist and fur warden for the US Bureau of Biological Survey, with an assignment to study caribou. Murie, then thirty-two, a World War I veteran, had already made two expeditions into the Canadian sub-Arctic in 1914 and 1917, collecting specimens and researching for the Carnegie Museum.

In 1921, he built a corral to capture caribou at the head of the Savage River in what was then known as Mount McKinley National Park (now Denali). In an effort to improve the strength and stamina of Alaska's imported reindeer herds, the caribou were bred with reindeer on a limited, experimental basis. Margaret "Mardy" Thomas, age twenty-one, visited the camp with her family in late July 1923. The two had met previously in Fairbanks. "At the end of five days of tramping about in a rosy haze in those enchanted mountains," Mardy wrote, "we both knew there was no life for us except together." On August 18, 1924, Olaus and Margaret were married in a log mission at Anvik on the bank of the Yukon River.

Between 1920 and 1926, Murie, often accompanied by Mardy after they were married, conducted an exhaustive study of Alaskan caribou, mapping migratory routes and estimating numbers. In 1927, he was assigned to study the Jackson Hole, Wyoming, elk herd, resulting in the classic publication *The Elk of North America*. His research on elk and coyotes broke new ground in the understanding of predator-prey relationships. In an era of intense eradication, his argument that a healthy predator population was key to ensuring a harmonious balance between them and their prey was highly controversial.

Olaus's younger half brother, Adolph "Ade" Murie, first came north to Alaska in 1921 to assist in the effort to capture caribou. In 1934, the younger Murie was hired on with the Wildlife Division of the National Park Service, three years later publishing *Ecology of the Coyote in Yellowstone*, which bolstered his brother's findings and inflamed the debate over predator eradication. In 1939, he returned to Alaska and began a three-year investigation into the relationship between wolves and their prey, which resulted in the publication of *The Wolves of Mount McKinley* in 1944. The book was hailed as the first in-depth examination of these relationships, but many people hotly condemned his landmark research for minimizing the impact of wolves on game animals; one prominent conservationist of the era called it "pseudo-science."

The Denali National Park wolf study, started by Murie and continued by various biologists, is one of the longest ongoing wolf studies in the world. Researchers L. David Mech and Layne Adams initiated a collaring project in Denali in early 1986, and it has run continuously since. More than four hundred wolves have been captured and collared.

"The presence of the wolf adds immeasurable richness and a wilderness spirit to the landscape," wrote Ade Murie. "One not need see a wolf to benefit from his presence. . . . It is enough to know that the wolf makes his home in this beautiful wilderness."

ON THE PEAKS ABOVE the Coleen and Sheenjek, where patches of bare ground dotted the south-facing hillsides and meltwater plunged toward both rivers, hardy Pasque flowers swayed in the breeze. Golden eagles, having returned from southern wintering areas, circled the summits seeking ptarmigan camouflaged in the rocks. A few ground squirrels, fresh out of hibernation, skittered their alarm calls as the Wanderer trotted by on the trails carved by caribou. The wind carried the scent of grizzly bears, awake from their long winter sleep. Now he had more competition to consider; the scent of winterkill was irresistible to bears and wolves alike.

He'd already traversed the territory of many other wolves, crossing the tracks and trails of hunting wolves several times on his journey into the snowy mountains. Each time, he stopped to investigate the scent, looking for clues that would alter his journey and life. Each splash of urine revealed hints as to the gender of the maker and the possibility of a mate and perhaps warned of danger. Sometimes he added his urine to the mix. He could've howled to signal a potential mate, or answered distant howls, but that would have betrayed his location when he most needed stealth. So far, he'd been adept—or lucky—enough to avoid potentially violent contact.

Late breakup and fierce storms sometimes delay or alter the direction of the caribou migration, and this year was no different. In most years, they migrated up both the Coleen and Sheenjek Rivers, but because of a tardy breakup north of the Porcupine, the herds veered to the east, seeking easier going and exposed forage. Even in optimal conditions, the journey exacts a physical toll on caribou, and fatigue and injury are common. There are always more miles to cross with no time to recuperate. Many stragglers die en route, feeding countless meat eaters.

As the days slipped by, the migration intensified. Long skeins of caribou streamed up the Coleen and many more on the Firth River in the northeast. The Wanderer, constantly in search of food, tested several and ignored others. Wolves seem to be able to quickly weigh their chances to determine if a chase will produce a meal or result in wasted energy or injury. Even in the best situations, most chases come up empty. On the open slopes and tundra north of the tree line, the Wanderer was almost always exposed and easily spotted by traveling or resting herds. The terrain, however, was broken and rocky, the folds and drainages providing cover that he used to draw close to his quarry before initiating a charge.

As he moved farther into the rugged mountains, the Wanderer exerted more energy, apparently without acquiring the nutrition to compensate. Likely he caught an unwary ptarmigan or two or tore at the bones of old winterkills, but he needed more. Beyond the tree line, there was no shelter from the weather. Bitter winds of nascent storms broke over the hills and valleys, heavy and laden with freezing rains. Periodic snow squalls cloaked the summits, then evaporated hours later under bright sun. One moment the Wanderer flinched against the pounding wind, and the next he floundered in sun-softened snow.

The Wanderer again crossed the Coleen and passed over the Continental Divide to the headwaters of the Firth River, moving fifty-five air miles in two days. To get there, he'd trespassed through other wolves' home ranges, as well as the trapping territory of Heimo Korth and his family, among the few permanent residents of the Arctic National Wildlife Refuge. In another season, baited traps would have awaited him.

Korth came to Alaska from Wisconsin in his twenties and met his wife, Edna, a Yupik Eskimo, in Savoonga on Saint Lawrence Island. Far above the Arctic Circle, in weather that would daunt most people, they built their own log cabins and lead a life that is the almost iconic embodiment of the Alaska dream. They've spent decades living on the Coleen River, raising a family in a subsistence lifestyle of trapping, hunting, fishing, and gathering.

He was one of many young men who set out for Alaska in the 1960s and 1970s to recreate the life of pioneer trappers and traders, but Korth is one of few who persisted in this venture. Along the way, he became a celebrity, complete with a Facebook fan club page. First came a book, *The Final Frontiersman: Heimo Korth and His Family, Alone in Alaska's Arctic Wilderness*, then video productions: *Braving Alaska* and *Surviving Alone in Alaska*. Others followed, including the Discovery series *The Last Alaskans*, which premiered in 2015. The show described Korth as "the celebrated godfather of the final frontier." All his public exposure doesn't lessen the hard work, skill, and endurance needed to lead the subsistence life of a trapper in this remote wilderness.

IN THE HEADWATERS OF THE FIRTH, caribou were increasingly abundant and a powerful lure for the young wolf, but he was finding them difficult to catch. Because they evolved with wolves, much of their behavior developed as a result of that relationship. It was their association with wolves that shaped their gregarious movements as a defense against attack. Caribou employ other strategies to avoid them as well. Recent research shows that caribou can detect wolves on snow with the aid of UV light. Because wolf fur absorbs UV light and snow reflects it, they appear dark to caribou, thus stripping even all-white wolves of their camouflage against the snow.

To date, the Wanderer had fared poorly in his hunts. At top speed, a caribou can run thirty miles per hour, and he'd struggled, and failed, to overtake healthy adults. Over good ground, he could match or even exceed their speed, but only for short bursts, not extended chases. Calving season, however, was only a few short days away, and the vulnerable newborns would be easy prey for a desperate wolf.

The Wanderer continued on, passing through the heart of the eastern Brooks Range. On May 16, he made a kill, either a sheep or a caribou, high on the north slope of Peak 4262. Two days later, five miles to the north, he made another kill, or found carrion, on the frozen margin of Joe Creek, a major tributary of the Firth River and just three miles from the border.

Four days later, he again crossed into Canada, descending to the upper reaches of the Firth. He was now in Ivvavik National Park, 250 miles as the raven flies north of the Yukon River. Through constant travel, risky moves, and fruitless detours, the Wanderer had emerged into the very heart of the Porcupine Herd's spring calving grounds. Freshly broken trails and vivid scents had lured him to the boreal ridges and tundra slopes where more than one hundred thousand caribou were now converging. Even a sore and weary wolf traversing unknown country should be able to find food here, though the competition could be dangerous.

7

Yukon: Land of the Midnight Sun

Spring is the best time of year in the north, both for people and animals. Moderate temperatures and increasing daylight vanquish the snow; rivers rage with runoff as if impatient for open, wild-flowing water. When the wind dies, the warm sun eases bodies long tensed against the cold. A vernal blush colors the catkins swaying in the breeze, and Pasque flowers bloom on south-facing slopes. Seldom is it quiet. The first insects buzz in the sun and the calls of varied thrush echo in the trees.

At no other time of year is there as much life in the taiga and on the tundra. Great flocks of geese and ducks whistle down on the thawing lakes and ponds, their throng soon joined by a multitude of breeding shorebirds and songbirds. By early June, the first broods of ptarmigan peck for food in the willows, and grouse chicks totter in the forest. Hare leverets sit and blink in the bright light. Moose and caribou calves trail their mothers; Dall sheep lambs traverse the talus. Foxes, coyotes, and wolves give birth, and tiny bear cubs emerge from natal dens. In trees or on cliffs, great horned owls, golden eagles, and peregrine falcons tend to their hatchlings.

The incredible surge in life is leveraged to take full advantage of summer's brief bounty and offer sufficient time for the young to grow strong before winter again grips the land. Spring's munificence also provides an abundance of prey for predators, especially so for a lone wolf entering unknown country. Hungry meat eaters aren't picky; they'll devour whatever they catch or find—it's all food.

In the mountains of northeast Alaska and northern Yukon Territory, however, winter refused to relinquish its hold. The Wanderer's swift journey north led him into Ivvavik National Park and back into snow squalls and subfreezing temperatures. The rocky, austere paths he traversed offered little shelter from the northeast winds. And the sun, even though it circled the steel-gray sky for more than twenty-two hours, had no power; only the month's end would bring temperatures into the upper forties. These mountains were carved by the cold—hewn by wind and ice, freeze and thaw—and for much of the year devoid of life. Now, the scent of countless caribou propelled the Wanderer northeast, deeper into the Firth River valley. On the high trails he followed, crusty snow and coarse stones bruised his pads, yet he never slowed, driven ever onward.

Ivvavik was the first Canadian national park established as a result of an Aboriginal lands claim, protecting a vital portion of the Porcupine Herd's calving grounds and migration routes. In the language of the region's Inuit, *Ivvavik* translates as "a place for giving birth; a nursery."

The British Mountains, part of the Brooks Range, run east to west through Ivvavik, paralleling the Arctic coast, and are sparsely vegetated save for small woody plants, isolated timber, lichens, grasses, and sedges. Several large rivers, notably the Firth and Babbage, cleave the ramparts on their rush to the Arctic Ocean. In its initial stages, the Firth, geologically the oldest river in Canada, tumbles down out of the mountains before slowing to wend through a broad tundra valley. Fringes of timber line the river bottom, but the wiry spruce and poplar disappear altogether nearer the coast. Extensive sheets of aufeis persist throughout the year, never thawing. During breakup, meltwater roars down the steep canyons, and tumbling boulders clack like distant thunder. The spring flood threatens even the strongest adult caribou who attempt to cross the Firth and often spells certain death for spring calves that follow.

The Wanderer's venture into Yukon Territory mirrored the main thrust of the Porcupine Herd toward its calving grounds. The Firth and the Coleen are two of the major routes followed annually by tens of thousands of caribou pushing north to the Arctic coastal plain. Most years, the migration trends through the mountains into Alaska on the Coleen, but the cold spring pushed it northeast into Yukon Territory on the Firth. In response to a plethora of factors—snow depth, temperature, wind strength and direction, exposed forage, and perhaps even the scent of a vast herd on the horizon—the caribou were coalescing in Ivvavik.

To date, the stable weather had favored the migration into the Firth River valley. At the end of April, a large segment of the herd had gathered far to the south in Yukon Territory and began moving north. Some years it takes more than two months to travel the four hundred miles between the southern winter range and the far-northern calving grounds. The life of a caribou is marked by perpetual movement as it loops far and wide over its territory, some individuals roaming as much as three thousand miles a year, one of the longest terrestrial migrations on earth.

Bad weather and deep snow can also impede migration; the cold spring in northeast Alaska had not stalled it but bent it eastward in response to the late thaw. When the journey is slowed by weather, calving begins in the mountains, with many calves lost to accidents, weather, and predation. This year, long strings of caribou streamed through the passes and down into the Firth River valley, moving with more urgency as calving approached. The pregnant cows had forged far ahead of the trailing bulls, exploiting any advantage the terrain offered: frozen rivers, windblown ridges, old trails—anywhere the hard-packed snow supported their weight. Given the rugged terrain between their seasonal habitats, they'd moved swiftly and efficiently. In deep snow, caribou, like wolves, conserve energy by walking single file, leaders trading off to conserve strength. Lured by the tantalizing smell of prey, the Wanderer hunted the multitude of trails they carved out.

In the early days of their journey, the bulk of the herd had vacated the flats southeast of the Porcupine River and moved into the mountains. Now, as calving time drew near, they had already negotiated the territories of five to ten resident packs, thirty to sixty wolves in all, each pack exacting a lethal toll. In Ivvavik, they moved into the realm of another type of wolf: the tundra wolf, one of two distinct ecological types of gray wolf identified by Canadian researchers. Tundra wolves roam mainly above the tree line and make long-distance seasonal shifts in territory to follow caribou; taiga wolves, like the wolves of Yukon-Charley, occupy smaller, discrete territories below the tree line, hunting moose year-round.

Wolves are never abundant in Ivvavik, but in spring their numbers correlate to the availability of caribou: greater numbers of the latter mean greater numbers of the former. Tundra wolves have adapted to the scarcity and seasonal abundance of prey by shifting their home range to follow transient caribou and by developing a social tolerance of other wolves that hunt the same prey. Because extreme northern Yukon Territory and Alaska support only limited and scattered pockets of wintering moose, Dall sheep, and muskox, there is no ecological advantage for tundra-dwelling wolves to stay and defend prey resources from other wolves.

The Wanderer had most likely crossed paths with other wolves who hunted or trailed the caribou. The exact nature of his interactions is unknown, but his innate tendency to avoid strange wolves would have been tempered by the urge to pair up and form his own pack. Tundra wolves appear to be more tolerant of unrelated wolves than those in the south tend to be. Because the overall density of wolves in the Arctic is low, compared to more southerly populations, and competition for space is lower, with greater territorial overlap, conditions appear optimal for dispersing tundra wolves to form new breeding pairs. In addition, their dispersal rate is higher and covers longer distances when compared to subarctic wolves. The Wanderer likely stood a good chance of finding an unrelated female to pair up with in Yukon.

Tundra wolves were once believed to be more likely to carry disease than wolves living in the south. More recent research suggests the opposite. A collaborative study by National Park Service biologists Mathew Sorum, of Yukon-Charley; Bridget Borg, of Denali; and two dozen other scientists revealed that the farther wolves lived from people, and their dogs, the fewer canine viruses and parasites they carried, and the healthier they were.

In two days of steady travel from the border, the Wanderer had followed Joe Creek downstream to its confluence with the Firth River. Just above the junction, the creek slows; its braided channels are favored by crossing caribou, even at high water. Below Joe Creek, the Firth narrows and carves through extensive canyons. Where it emerges onto the coastal plain, the river wanders, forming a wide delta where it enters the Beaufort Sea just west of Herschel Island.

The Wanderer crossed Joe Creek near its mouth and then negotiated the much larger, ice-choked Firth. Caribou in both small bands and large groups continued to flood out of the south and west and into the valley, where they paused to forage on the windswept slopes and tundra. Snow-fall had been relatively light, and wide swaths of exposed ground provided needed food for the pregnant cows. But they were not the only migrants here. Small flocks of snow buntings pecked for seeds. Overhead a few golden eagles searched for newborn calves and unwary rodents, as did jaegers who darted over the ridges.

The Wanderer continued into the higher summits southeast of the river, directly in the path of the massive herd, but instead of lingering, he kept moving southeast through the mountains, opposite the flow of caribou heading north. Some fifty miles east of the Alaska border, the Wanderer reached the south side of 2,975-foot Mount Sedgwick and trotted straight into danger. For decades—perhaps even centuries—wolves had denned on Sedgwick and at three other sites to the north on the Trail River. Perhaps some ancient, obscure path led the Wanderer here.

Because young pups are extremely vulnerable to predators, any strange wolf that approaches an active den is vigorously attacked by the resident pack and likely killed. Even grizzlies retreat from this unrelenting attack. But unguarded dens are clearly at risk. In one incident south of Mount Sedgwick, a grizzly killed four pups at the unprotected Berry Creek Den. If the Sedgwick Den was occupied, the Wanderer somehow escaped contact, ghosting by, just out of sight and scent.

He next continued southeast, crossed the Babbage River at the eastern boundary of Ivvavik, and trotted into a wide pass between Welcome and Sleepy Mountains in the Barn Mountains, the far eastern portion of the Brooks Range. In a single day, he'd covered twenty-two miles, traversing folded mountains and the thawing river. He spent the afternoon of May 26 resting on a barren, sun-splashed 2,200-foot knob in the center of the pass. Throughout his rambles, the Wanderer seemed to prefer the high country, a terrain similar to his home territory in Yukon-Charley.

On May 28, the Wanderer moved another twenty-five air miles east, crossing the Blow River to a prominence near Skull Ridge in the foothills of the Richardson Mountains, where large numbers of caribou often winter but were now long gone. He'd crossed into the territory of the Blow River Pack, on occasion the largest in the region, a perilous foray. He'd also reached what would be his farthest point east, less than thirty miles from the Beaufort Sea and the mouth of the Mackenzie River, or *Kuukpak*, literally "great river" in Inuit. The weather that day in Aklavik, the nearest Inuit village, was fair, 59°F, with negligible wind. In only one short week, spring had come to the Arctic, and the snow rapidly melted in the bright sun.

Despite abundant prey and the energy demands of mountain travel, the Wanderer had yet to make a significant kill in Yukon Territory. After having left the valley of the Firth, and then traveling directly through large groups of caribou going the opposite way, what drove him east? Why didn't he stop to hunt the animals moving past? Or did he try, but fail? Far to the northwest, calving had begun on the Firth, but the Wanderer was now almost ninety air miles away. Hundreds, if not thousands, of newborns were dropping into the world there daily. Why did he follow the caribou's *backtrail* instead of following them north? Had encounters with other wolves dictated his movements?

The Wanderer next made a radical, rather puzzling, course change. Instead of heading back the way he'd come, he loped southwest thirty miles, as the raven flies, to the headwaters of Black Fox Creek in Vuntut National Park. This park, established in 1995 as part of the Vuntut Gwitchin First Nations Final Agreement with the Canadian government, protects portions of the Porcupine Herd's spring and fall migration routes and the lifeways of the Vuntut Gwich'in, "people of the lakes," who have lived here for countless generations. The park abuts Ivvavik National Park to the north and is cooperatively managed by Parks Canada, the Vuntut Gwich'in government, and the North Yukon Renewable Resources Council. The park has two contrasting regions: the Old Crow Flats, a network of over two thousand shallow lakes, and the rolling foothills and scattered peaks of the southern British Mountains.

In Vuntut, just north of Old Crow Flats, the Wanderer was again below the timberline, where the boreal forest was burgeoning with life. Plants shed their subsurface dormancy, thrusting through the soil and into the light. Lapland diapensia, bluebells, lady's slippers, and other early flowering plants brightened the understory. In the meadows between wildfire-scorched timber, hawk owls hunted darting rodents. Vast flights of waterfowl winged overhead on their way to nesting grounds on the Old Crow Flats or farther north. As white-crowned sparrows and robins sang in the trees, tiny moose calves wobbled in the shadows. Grizzlies and black bears rumbled through the forest and mountain slopes in search of winterkill, peavine, and willow roots. And the resident wolves, taiga wolves, were on the move, hunting the freshening bounty. One pack denned near Black Fox Creek and jealously guarded its territory.

Wolves often prefer prey species that provide the safest, most efficient meal—say, caribou over moose, or elk over bison. Although taiga wolves hunt moose year-round, they switch to caribou when the herd passes through their range. In contrast, tundra wolves have few alternatives to caribou because there are few other large prey animals north of the tree line. With the caribou gone to the far north, moose were again the resident wolves' principal prey, and they would not tolerate competition. The Wanderer needed to be on guard.

A number of factors could have influenced his next move. Perhaps an encounter with the resident pack sent him fleeing. Or maybe the memory of passing caribou turned him back to the northwest. Whatever the cause, he took off. In one incredible day, he traveled over forty-five air miles northwest, crossed the headwaters of the flooding Babbage River, and reached Muskeg Creek, a tributary of the Firth in the middle of the British Mountains. And just like that, he caught up with the trailing edge of the migration.

On the last day of May, on a tundra slope of a rocky escarpment just east of the Firth River, in an area he'd passed through just days before, the Wanderer brought down an adult caribou, finally breaking his long fast. For the next three days, he rested and feasted on his kill, gulping down the choice organs first, followed by the muscle and congealed blood. His long, convoluted jaunt, running a gauntlet of varied threats, gave life to the old Russian adage "A wolf is kept fed by his feet."

Through the first week of June, the Wanderer coursed the uplands just south of the Firth's tortuous gorge. A large segment of the herd had moved north into the Buckland Hills bordering the coastal plain, but hundreds more lingered on the snow-free slopes, trailing tiny newborns. Now the loitering bulls, their tall, velvet-covered antlers waving with each step, began to catch up to the main group. Within a few weeks, the entire herd would gather along the coast. For a lone wolf, the hunting could not be better.

Caribou give birth to a single, precocious calf, weighing about thirteen pounds. Immediately after calving, which takes about an hour, the mother thoroughly smells and vigorously licks her calf clean, forging a powerful bond. Once imprinted, cow and calf can recognize each other by scent alone even in a herd of thousands. Almost at once, the calf struggles to stand and support itself on spindly legs. In minutes, it takes its first tottering steps. Newborns are able to run and follow their mothers within a few hours of birth. Nurtured by their mother's rich milk, calves grow rapidly, doubling their weight in ten to fifteen days.

With about 80 to 90 percent of mature females in the herd pregnant, thousands of calves are born on peak days, most over a two-week span, swamping the local predators. The "calving spurt," as biologists call it, improves survival rates. Until they are about two weeks old, calves are relatively easy for a wolf to catch. If calving took place over an extended period of time, predators could pick them off one by one. Mass calving allows many more to mature before being tested by wolves or bears, and the vulnerability of calves declines markedly with each passing week.

The odds favored the Wanderer in pursuit of a calf. He was simply faster and stronger. Even though calves stick close to their mothers when pursued, that proximity offers little protection. Unlike moose cows, which vigorously defend their calves, caribou cows are incapable of meaningful defense. How many calves the Wanderer took down over the next week is unknown, but judging by his movements, the hunting was good.

Research on predation rates by wolves in the Porcupine Herd's winter range indicates that each wolf takes about thirty caribou per year. Migratory packs kill an estimated 3 to 5 percent of the Porcupine Herd each year but appear not to be a primary factor limiting its size.

On June 9, the Wanderer abandoned the upper Firth and loped twenty-five miles north through the mountains, crossed the Firth at its confluence with Canyon Creek, and stopped on a high point just west of where the river emerges onto the coastal plain. The north-facing foothills were slowly thawing, but still pounded by cold northeast winds. The terrain bore the scars of passing caribou: trails trampled under countless hooves; acres of black raisin-sized droppings; molted hair; and shed antlers, not needed for protection during pregnancy. Hundreds of animals grazed the ridges to the east.

The next day, the Wanderer moved another twenty miles to the northwest, crossed the Malcolm River, and reached Fish Creek, in the core of the Yukon Territory's portion of the calving grounds and just four air miles from the Beaufort Sea. He may have reached the Arctic strand and peered out across the frozen sea ice before turning back. Perhaps he even caught a whiff of a polar bear. Everywhere, the distinctive odor of wet, shedding caribou hair drifted on the wind.

For a lone wolf, the scents, sounds, and sights on the coastal plain must have constituted sensory overload. The smell of caribou was rich, strong, and ubiquitous. Here on the plain—the realm of the lemming, snowy owl, Arctic fox, muskox, and land-denning polar bear—the tundra shook off the snow and cold to welcome not only the arrival of the herd, as many as 170,000, but migrating birds in the tens of thousands.

The Porcupine Herd's calving grounds edging the Beaufort Sea extend more than one hundred miles along the Arctic coastal plain, with a small portion in Yukon Territory and the remainder in Alaska. Conditions are almost ideal for calving and calf survival. Wolves and bears are relatively few, and late green-up provides a month-long reprieve from the impending mosquito hatch. Located between the mountains and sea, the coastal plain is an expanse of relatively flat, poorly drained tundra influenced by the sea's cooling effects. Snow and ice persist on the plain until late May or early June, but even then, the sea remains frozen longer. Permafrost traps and holds water at the surface, the five inches of annual precipitation resulting in vast tracts of standing water and abundant forage. The tundra is perfect for mosquito rearing and, in turn, nesting birds that feast on insects. Throughout the summer, ice floes and pack ice linger offshore, with cool winds and damp fog blowing in on the northeast wind. The prevailing wind is a crucial factor on the calving grounds, cooling a long summer of continuous daylight.

On June 11, during the peak of calving season, the Wanderer made another inexplicable move. Forsaking the abundant prey he'd located, he trotted twenty-five miles west to the Clarence River, just south of Demarcation Bay in Alaska. Perhaps a pack of wolves had driven him out, or he'd followed a few small groups of caribou trickling west. Then again, maybe the lure of far, blue horizons pushed him onward. Now back in Alaska, the Wanderer once more entered unknown country alone, hungry, and vulnerable.

8

"The Sacred Place Where Life Begins"

The Wanderer moved quickly on his second day back in Alaska, trotting thirty air miles west to the Ekaluakat River in the northern foothills of the Brooks Range. He traversed hard-packed drifts, expansive sheets of aufeis, and wide swaths of rolling tussocks; he flushed shorebirds and waterfowl clustered on small patches of bare tundra and slices of open water. Everywhere, the haunting laugh of long-tailed ducks wafted over the leads. Time and again, jaegers screamed down out of the steel-gray sky, harrying him from their nesting territories.

As he loped west, a vast expanse sprawled before him. Alaska's portion of the coastal plain is more extensive than in Yukon Territory. The Alaska segment stretches sixty miles wide from the sea on its northern edge to the summits of the Brooks Range on the south, containing a variety of riparian and wetland habitats. In Yukon Territory, the plain varies from eighteen miles wide in the east to just six miles in the west.

By June 13, the Wanderer had crossed the tundra to within four miles of the Aichilik River. In the rest of Alaska, summer had unfolded, but on the coast, spring had barely begun. In the Arctic, a few short miles can make a huge difference in weather. Just west of the Canadian border, the temperature was 34°F, with a biting northeast wind. Snowmelt was late and open water scarce. A short distance to the south in the higher foothills, it was in the upper 50s, the wind negligible. On the plain, the nearly continuous daylight had yet to trigger widespread melt, but in the tundra uplands, the first grasses and wildflowers pushed into the light. Blackish oxytrope and purple mountain saxifrage, the first in a sequence of blooming Arctic plants, grew in low, dense mats that absorb and hold in warmth, an adaptation to the cool and fickle spring temperatures. Fine hairs sprouted on the stems and buds of wooly lousewort, helping retain warm air around the young plants. On the North Slope, the Wanderer had entered an even more austere and challenging landscape than his natal terrain.

Moving deeper into the Arctic National Wildlife Refuge, the Wanderer encountered fewer and fewer caribou. The bulk of the herd had cohered well behind him. In most springs, hundreds would be filtering past his current location, headed toward the heart of the calving grounds around the Jago and Okpilak Rivers. Despite the lack of caribou, other migrants arrived daily in dizzying numbers and array.

With abundant habitat and feed, more than a million birds—two hundred different species in all—nest on the coastal plain. Thanks to the underlying permafrost, in places up to 2,100 feet thick, the tundra is pocked with countless ponds and lakes. Ironically, the North Slope is a dry desert with fewer than five inches of annual precipitation, yet it has widespread standing water due to poor drainage. The freeze-thaw action on the different soil types and substrates creates landforms distinctive to permafrost terrain: hummocks, tussocks, frost boils, pingos, and polygons. Along the coast, a series of shallow lagoons, up to a mile or so wide and fringed with low-lying barrier islands and sandbars, offer additional nesting grounds for a variety of waterfowl and shorebirds.

The immense productivity and unparalleled habitat in summer attract birds from far and wide, some undertaking journeys spanning thousands of miles. Buff-breasted sandpipers, numbering fewer than twenty thousand worldwide, fly here from Argentina to court and nest. Tiny Baird's sandpipers, weighing less than one and a half ounces, also arrive from South America, flying the entire 9,300-mile journey in as little as five weeks. And the champion migrator, the Arctic tern, commutes twenty thousand miles round-trip between Alaska and the Antarctic every year, the longest migration of any animal on earth. Familiar northern species like tundra swans, Pacific loons, king eiders, and snow geese can also be found here. Beyond the lagoons, strings of scoters and long-tailed ducks fly back and forth across the shallow waters of the Beaufort Sea. Eurasian wigeons, ivory gulls, smews, and other transients also make infrequent stops in this protected area. Common shorebirds like red-necked phalaropes, ruddy turnstones, and semipalmated sandpipers arrive in abundance. After all the effort the birds expend to cross the long miles, court, breed, and nest, many eggs and hatchlings fall prey to varied predators, including wolves. A trekker once observed a wolf devouring the eggs of a tundra swan, despite the swan pair's attempts to drive it off.

As the Wanderer moved west, resident willow and rock ptarmigan seemed to vanish. Coming through the mountains back in mid-May, the wolf had located ptarmigan easily. The cocks had preened and crowed openly, advertising for hens and defending their territories. They appeared oblivious to all but their task of luring a hen, but that was a deception. The birds understood the threat presented by eagles, gyrfalcons, and foxes and never lost awareness of movement. For the most part, the breeding birds had teased rather than fed the hungry wolf. Now, ptarmigan were well concealed in the thickets, a few still on their nests, most shepherding their broods to shelter. As he traveled, the Wanderer scoured the plain for rodents, in addition to the migratory birds and their eggs. But the tiny meals would assuage his hunger only temporarily. He needed to kill a caribou, lap blood, and feel meat burn in his belly. To survive, and thrive, the Wanderer required the vast herds, but they were absent here, the vulnerable calves miles away.

The wolf stopped on a tundra prominence west of the Aichilik to scent the wind and study the terrain. Nearby, a short-eared owl peered at him from a tussock mound. On a distant inland ridge, a tiny band of bull caribou pawed through the snow for forage. Of the Arctic National Wildlife Refuge's 30,136 square miles, the wolf had entered the critical heart: the core calving grounds of the Porcupine Herd, a place the Gwich'in call *Iizhik Gwats'an Gwandaii Goodlit*, "the sacred place where life begins." Spread out before the wolf was not just a biome peppered with life but one of the most contentious pieces of real estate in North America: the refuge's infamous "1002 area." The Wanderer had arrived in search of food, a territory of his own, and a potential mate. Caribou gathered to feed and give birth, as they had for centuries. Neither species knew of, or sought, the incandescent controversy that threatened them.

GEOLOGISTS HAVE IDENTIFIED THE "1002" as possibly holding large oil reserves, much of which lie directly beneath the calving grounds. When President Carter signed ANILCA into law in December 1980, expanding the Arctic National Wildlife Refuge from 8.9 million acres to 19.3 million acres (an area nearly the size of South Carolina), most of the original refuge was designated as wilderness, except for approximately 1.5 million acres on the coastal plain. Section 1002 of ANILCA mandated an inventory and assessment of fish and wildlife resources in the area and an analysis of the potential impacts of oil and gas exploration and development. Drilling in the 1002 would be allowed only with congressional authorization.

Much of the debate over development revolves around the value of the economically recoverable oil versus the potential harm to wildlife. In 1998, the US Geological Survey released its "Arctic National Wildlife Refuge, 1002 Area, Petroleum Assessment." The agency's midrange estimate of the oil reserves rose from 13.8 billion barrels to 20.7 billion barrels. Critics charged that the increase was unscientific and politically motivated. Today, despite high gas prices, a shift toward alternative energy sources casts doubt on the economic viability of drilling in the 1002.

As early as the mid-1960s, Alaska Natives protested federal plans for oil and gas lease sales on Alaska's North Slope. During the decades-long, often bitter and divisive fight over 1002 oil development, no one has fought against it harder than the Gwich'in, especially the people of Arctic Village.

Arctic Village, established in 1909, is home to the Neets'aii Gwich'in, "residents of the north side." The village is on traditional lands on the east fork of the Chandalar River on the southwestern edge of the refuge. Archaeological discoveries date human use of the area back thousands of years. Ancestors of the Neets'aii Gwich'in lived a highly nomadic life, using seasonal camps and semipermanent settlements to pursue fish and game. Many Gwich'in still live a way of life tied to the land of their forebears.

Caribou are the primary source of subsistence food in Arctic Village and a critical part of the Neets'aii Gwich'in cultural identity. Large segments of the Porcupine Herd travel past the village every year, and as they have for ages, the people hunt them for food and hides. For countless generations, caribou have sustained the Gwich'in communities all across the north. For the Gwich'in, oil development in the refuge threatens both caribou and their very way of life.

As the Gwich'in view it, they have nothing to gain and everything to lose from oil development. Some Gwich'in tribes in Alaska refused to participate in the Alaska Native Claims Settlement Act of 1971, instead maintaining ownership of 1.8 million acres of their traditional land. The people are proud of their decision.

Not all Alaska Natives oppose drilling in the 1002. The Iñupiat village of Kaktovik, located on Barter Island on the Beaufort Sea coast, straddles the divide between traditional and modern. Kaktovik, which in Iñupiaq means "seining place," was a traditional coastal fishing site until the late 1950s, when the village coalesced around the construction of a distant early warning radar station. The village began to change in earnest as oil revenues began to flow in the 1970s. The North Slope Borough, which spans much of Arctic Alaska, has prospered on oil taxes and supports Kaktovik with electricity and piped water and sewer services. There is a K–12 school, basketball gym, health clinic, public safety building, and fire station, as well as telephones, mail, public radio, and cable TV. In comparison, many Gwich'in villages lack basic infrastructure.

Subsistence is still an important part of life in Kaktovik and highly dependent upon the hunting of caribou, bowhead whales, birds, and seals. Residents of this isolated village are poised to be among the biggest beneficiaries of development but also to experience some of the biggest disruptions. Sharp divisions still linger in Kaktovik and other Iñupiat communities.

Prodrilling advocates proclaim that oil development can be carried out responsibly without harming the caribou. The Gwich'in call that non-sense because the Porcupine Herd births precisely where drilling would take place. The calving area in the refuge is narrower than around Prudhoe Bay, they say, and hemmed in by a mountain range and the Arctic Ocean, so the impacts would likely be greater. Proponents counter that the herds and oil can coexist, and point to caribou wandering the oil fields as visible proof. The Gwich'in respond that before development, the Central Arctic Herd calved all along the central coast but have had to shift their move-ments away from the oil infrastructure because of the commotion. Multi-ple studies have shown that pregnant cows are easily disturbed and avoid disruptive human activity in the oil fields. Conservationists also argue that the debate is not solely oil versus caribou but about the protection of the last undeveloped, pristine segment of America's Arctic coast and the critical denning sites of polar bears, a species at risk due to global climate change.

Until recently, the residents of fifteen Gwich'in villages scattered across northeast Alaska and northwest Canada and their allies were on the win-ning side of the drawn-out political battle in Washington, DC, over oil development in the refuge. They helped beat back repeated attempts in Congress to legalize drilling in the refuge's 1.6-million-acre coastal plain.

But on December 20, 2017, Congress approved legislation to open Alaska's 1002 area to oil and gas development. The Trump administration issued the first leases the following January. On President Joe Biden's first day in office, he issued an executive order for a temporary moratorium on drilling activity in the refuge. As long as the scent of big money is in the wind, the battle will go on.

AFTER ALL THE LONG, HARD MILES, chance, and the vagaries of his journey, the Wanderer had entered near-ideal hunting territory for a wolf in spring: the core calving grounds at the peak of birthing season around the Jago and Okpilak Rivers. In most years, it would be a perfect place to hunt and feast. But instead of plenty, he found famine.

If the caribou were here, they'd be obvious; they are hard to miss in calving season, which peaks in the first two weeks of June. The herds are alive with sound and movement. In rolling terrain, they often can be heard well before they are seen. The cows and calves call back and forth as they move over the tundra. Young calves strengthen themselves by racing in circles about their mothers or chasing other calves. They leap, jump, and shake their heads in play. Dodging pursuers is a continuous but important activity. Their sharp, abrupt turns at top speed not only build strength but also develop tactics for predator avoidance. Play, for young caribou and wolves alike, is key to honing coordination, strength, and agility. As they develop, calves will gather in "nursery" groups of up to a dozen or so and stray some distance from their mothers, but usually in the company of one or two cows. During play, the young calves may be more susceptible to predators than when they are close to their mothers.

There are thirty-two herds in Alaska; most utilize seasonal ranges and follow traditional migratory patterns, returning each spring to unique calving areas. A few small herds are nonmigratory. Long-distance migrations allow caribou to access whatever forage is seasonally most abundant and nutritious.

The Porcupine Herd's range encompasses almost one hundred thousand square miles of Yukon Territory and Alaska, but the coastal plain is essential to calving and calf survival. The coastal tundra supports an abundance of nutritious plants vital to the pregnant and nursing cows, especially after the long, lean winter. In most years, snowmelt and green-up on the plain coincide with calving, which gives the cows access to this food when they need it most. But not this spring. Due to the later than usual snowmelt, the majority of the herd remained in Yukon Territory. Wolves there partook of the bounty; perhaps the Wanderer should have lingered.

9

Heart of the Calving Grounds

Along with the abundance of preferred forage, the relative dearth of wolves on the coastal plain played a significant role in it becoming the herd's prime calving grounds. Some five to six packs, twenty to forty wolves in all, denned inland in the mountains and foothills along the refuge's major rivers: the Kongakut, Aichilik, Hulahula, Sadlerochit, Jago, and Canning. Given the immensity of the terrain, the wolf population was quite low, a result of limited prey. Each spring, hunters from the various packs coursed far and wide over the plain from their den sites in search of caribou. Even this far north, ravens, intent on pilfering from a kill, often trailed them.

The scarcity of wolves on the North Slope has been attributed to several factors, first and foremost being the brutal winters. Except for a few weeks each spring, when caribou typically provide an abundance of food, there's little for them to eat for long months on end. The few resident ungulates—sheep, muskox, and moose—live mostly in the mountains and are too few in number to support many wolves. Consequently, the diet of these northern wolves varies by season. When the Porcupine Herd is present, many of the mountain wolves venture onto the plain to hunt alone or in pairs. They kill relatively few adults during the calving season, but they take a substantial number of calves. After the caribou leave the coastal plain, the wolves return to the uplands to hunt other large prey. However, rodents, ground squirrels, and birds constitute a significant part of their year-round diet, as much as half of their summer fare.

The terrain itself is another important limiting factor. No one has ever found a wolf den on the coastal plain. Permafrost and abundant surface water prevent denning. Of eleven dens in the northern part of the Arctic refuge, one was in the foothills, and the others were located in the higher mountains. Predictably, the dens are in the center of each pack's territory and removed from conflict with other packs. A den on the plain itself, in the heart of the calving grounds, would be a great boon to a pack during the spring migration, but no such site exists.

Spring's bounty in the Arctic is short-lived, a few weeks at best before the caribou move on and the birds migrate south. Even if the Wanderer found a mate and somehow the pair denned on the plain, their pups would be unlikely to survive, the shortage of winter prey a critical issue on the tundra. Wolves have fairly large litters, but even in more hospitable habitats, most pups don't survive to adulthood. Pup survival is often about 50 percent and sometimes much lower, hovering between 10 and 20 percent in some areas. A variety of factors, such as disease, genetics, hunting success, and predation, influence litter size and survival rates.

Wolf pups need a lot of food, especially in late summer and early fall when they are nearing adult size, which coincides with the time when moose, sheep, and caribou are in their prime from eating high-quality forage. Their young are now strong and swift enough to evade the wolves. This is the leanest time of the year for pups and adults alike. The coastal plain in late autumn is devoid of the life that defines it in spring. Consequently, it is the season when many wolves die of starvation.

A few researchers believe that North Slope wolf populations were once artificially depressed due to aerial hunting. The vast, nearly flat, snow-covered tundra is ideal for finding and chasing them down with a plane. Beginning back in the 1950s, when sport hunting for polar bears was still legal, some guides offered late-winter combination bear-and-wolf hunts. The technique for both animals was similar. Small planes, usually Piper Super Cubs, flying in tandem would seek out tracks and follow them to the quarry. With polar bears, one plane would fly on ahead, land on the ice, sometimes miles offshore, and disgorge the hunters to wait while the other plane drove the bear to them. Wolves were simply tracked and shotgunned from the air. In the decades since, these practices have been prohibited, but judging by a few notorious violations and infrequent rumors, the illegal take has not died out completely.

The limited prey base of the coastal plain also holds down the tundra grizzly population. Thus, the two principal predators of caribou calves are relatively scarce on the coastal tundra. In more southerly regions, bear predation would be more intense.

Another factor played a part in the evolution of the coastal plain as calving grounds: the late emergence of insects. Insects hatch on the plain almost a month later than on the south side of the Brooks Range. Mosquitoes in the Arctic are an immutable force and affect all living creatures, especially large warm-blooded animals. Meltwater trapped at the surface by the underlying frozen ground makes for perfect mosquito habitat. According to entomologists, a swarm of Arctic mosquitoes may contain hundreds of thousands, perhaps millions, of insects. The biomass of mosquitoes on the North Slope alone is said to be larger than that of all Arctic caribou combined; entomologists estimate the mosquito biomass in Alaska at ninety-six million pounds.

The insects emerge on the coastal plain in late June and early July and soon drive caribou to cool and windy coastal areas, even out into the shallow Beaufort Sea, to escape the torment. The problem becomes acute during warm, calm weather and whenever caribou forage through wet tundra, where the insects breed. Mosquitoes can drain as much as half a cup of blood each day from an adult caribou. Young calves are weakened by blood loss; some even die. The bugs can become abundant enough to prevent cows from nursing their young. Adults have been driven to the point of injury, or death, as they frantically attempt to escape these micropredators' unrelenting attacks, some reportedly dying due to asphyxiation from inhaling hundreds of mosquitoes as they flee. Without sufficient respite from mosquitoes, caribou may lose weight and weaken during a time of the year when they need to recoup from the migration, nurse their young, and fatten for the coming winter.

As a result of warming temperatures, mosquitoes are thriving. The insect plague worsens each year, lasting longer than ever before. With the Arctic warming twice as fast as the rest of the planet, the ponds where mosquitos breed now melt earlier than in the past, enabling an early hatch, thus allowing more and more to survive to adulthood. For the insects that traditional Iñupiat call *Kiktugiaq*, a changing climate means larger numbers and a longer life. Climate change has brought mosquito-emergence time closer to caribou-calving time. All the constant running back and forth to avoid insect harassment reduces opportunities to rest and feed, which are especially critical for pregnant and nursing mothers. That's bad news for both caribou and their principal predators.

Two other insects harass and torment caribou. Warble flies lay their eggs on the hairs of a caribou's legs and lower body. The eggs hatch into larvae, which then penetrate the skin and travel to the animal's back. The parasitic larvae grow there until early summer, when they break through the skin and drop to the ground to pupate in the soil. In some parts of the north, these flies are referred to as "heel flies" or "caribou grubs," and the larvae are called "wolves."

Buzzing swarms of botflies harass caribou too, also causing them to stop feeding and flee in panic. This pernicious pest deposits its larvae on

PREVIOUS PAGE: *The intense gaze of a winter wolf displays the strength, intelligence, and curiosity that combine to make it North America's apex predator.* **TOP LEFT:** *A small pack, traveling in typical single file, negotiates the wind-swept Yukon River.* (Courtesy of National Park Service) **TOP RIGHT:** *A wolf in a leg-hold trap set near a bait station remains motionless and silent as the trapper approaches.* **BOTTOM:** *Alaska's fur trapping heritage stretches back well into the 1800s.* (Courtesy of Eagle Historical Society)

In Canada's Ivvavik National Park, the Firth River, a major caribou migration corridor, often remains frozen well into caribou calving season in late May. (Courtesy of Parks Canada)

TOP: *Wolves howl to locate pack members, warn of danger, or convey other information.* **BOTTOM:** *Adults communicate with pups via body language as well as auditory signals about food when it is available and commands to seek shelter or follow.*

TOP LEFT: *When a wolf wears his short summer coat, a radio collar is quite visible. In winter, the collar is largely hidden under the thick neck ruff.* **TOP LEFT (BOTTOM):** *Biologists Bridget Borg and John Burch kneel by a sedated wolf while pilots Dennis Miller (left) and Rick Swisher (right) observe.* **TOP RIGHT:** *In the spectacular Yukon–Charley uplands, research pilot Terry Cambier holds the sedated all–white Step Mountain female 222.* **BOTTOM:** *John Burch perches on the skid as he aims a tranquilizer gun at a fleeing wolf.* (Top left photo by the author; all others courtesy of National Park Service)

TOP: *In periods of deep snow, prey animals, like these caribou, are more vulnerable to wolves who more easily move through the powder or across the crust.* **BOTTOM LEFT:** *A remote trail camera captures the interaction between wolves and a grizzly bear in Ivvavik National Park.* (Courtesy of Parks Canada) **BOTTOM RIGHT:** *A wolf in winter coat similar in color to Wolf 258, the Wanderer.*

TOP: *Late autumn is hungry season for wolves. In thin snow, a lone wolf is no match for an adult moose, especially a healthy bull.* **BOTTOM:** *A little over six months—and nearly 3,000 miles after leaving Yukon-Charley—the Wanderer came to rest under a gnarled spruce on the banks of the Kanuti River.* **FOLLOWING PAGE:** *Tracks of a hunting wolf lead into the high mountains.*

the snout. The larvae then wriggle into the caribou's mouth, then nasal sinuses and back of the throat, where they spend the winter in a cluster near the base of the tongue. Larvae infestations block and irritate the nostrils, tormenting the host; they sneeze and snort as they try to alleviate the discomfort. The maturing larvae can cause pneumonia and, in extreme cases, even suffocation. Ultimately, they detach themselves from their host and are sneezed out in the spring, where they fall to the ground to pupate and develop into adults. In the fall, the cycle begins again.

Given the obvious torment and threat insects pose in the Arctic, the benefit from an extra month's respite from them cannot be overestimated. The late hatch, combined with low pressure from predators, cool temperatures, and abundant forage, makes the coastal plain nearly ideal for calving.

Every year in early July, caribou come together in mass gatherings after calving, often numbering in the thousands, even tens of thousands. The bulls and immature adults that trailed the spring migration join up with the cows and calves already on the plain. These spectacular, tightly bunched aggregations rival the great assemblages of grazing animals that seasonally roam the African savannah. These aggregations, known in eastern Canada as *La Foule*, "the throng," form in response to the insects' harassment, although some biologists point to an ill-defined social purpose. In addition to minimizing the tormenting insects, the tight bunches are likely to thwart predators because they are able to detect danger earlier, allowing them more time to feed intensively. But these massed herds quickly deplete local forage. The assemblages also pound marshy areas into mud, often trampling bird's nests and hatchlings, and exposing those that survive to foxes, jaegers, and circling hawks. A field biologist once saw a caribou eating the nests and hatchlings.

The aggregations don't last long, and the mosquito plague soon drives many into the foothills and mountains in search of high, dry, and windy terrain, triggering the beginning of a general movement to the south.

RESIDENT WOLVES KNOW WELL the feeding locations and preferred habitat of their main prey species and are attuned to seasonal patterns, learning where and when to look. The Wanderer had no such advantage. He was an explorer, a wayfarer, a traveler, and a disperser. Lean times were part of the quest.

For the Wanderer, finding a mate and available territory was an enormous challenge, compounded this spring by the lack of food. Why didn't he turn back? Return to prey-rich Ivvavik? He could have retraced his steps and been amid the herd in two days' travel. The most likely answer: other wolves. Although it is impossible to know what influenced the Wanderer's journey in Ivvavik, it is certain that caribou calving had attracted multiple wolves. A loner like the Wanderer could not safely compete with roving packs or stay near them. Any kill he made would not remain secret as the scent would attract competitors.

Since leaving Ivvavik, the Wanderer seemed to be to living primarily on small prey. Two-pound Arctic ground squirrels likely provided him with several small meals, while voles and lemmings served as other snacks. To find adequate food, the Wanderer had to keep moving and cover huge swaths of country with his ground-eating trot. Growing desperate, he'd test and chase almost any animal he encountered.

Several times during the Wanderer's travels, he caught fleeting glimpses of Arctic foxes or heard their alarm barks. Wolves are notoriously intolerant of other canids. For an Arctic fox, a wolf is a traditional enemy to be strictly avoided. The Wanderer would kill any he surprised at close range or chased down. Although a fox would make a small meal, any contact would carry a special peril: rabies is always present in Arctic foxes on the northern and western coasts. Periodic epizootics spread the disease to dogs, wolves, and other animals.

An infected wolf eventually dies a terrible, lingering death, but it also poses a threat to other wolves and humans. A pack of nine wolves was found dead in northeastern Alaska during the spring of 1985, with five of the animals testing positive for rabies. In 1977, biologist Richard Chapman shot and killed a rabid wolf that attacked him in the Arctic refuge. The previous day, Chapman had seen it fighting with several of its pack mates. He later found the remains of six more; two tested positive. Other attacks on people by rabid wolves have been reported in both Canada and Alaska.

Over the course of the next two days, the Wanderer moved west from the foothills to the coastal plain beyond the Jago River, the usual center of calving activity, but this year nearly silent. Travel was not easy. Instead of winter's hard, wind-carved snow, the tepid thaw created a punchy, wet surface that irregularly collapsed underfoot, which strained muscles and ligaments, testing the wolf's overall endurance and strength.

He continued his journey west, moving forty-eight miles as the raven flies, almost overnight, crossing three Arctic rivers pulsing with rotting ice and meltwater to reach low benchland on the west side of Itkilyariak Creek, a tributary of the Sadlerochit River. The Itkilyariak flows north out of Sunset Pass in the Sadlerochit Mountains, the range of a resident wolf pack. Their den was well positioned to intercept caribou coming through the pass, a traditional migration corridor from the upper Sadlerochit River. The river's headwaters are dominated by two of the tallest peaks in the eastern Brooks Range, Mount Michelson, at 8,855 feet, and Mount Chamberlin, at 9,020 feet. Again, the Wanderer seemed to escape peril undetected.

Without discernible pause, the Wanderer kept going west, covering another twenty-seven miles. On June 17, after yet another twenty-five-mile jaunt, he crossed the Canning River, the northeastern boundary of the Arctic refuge. In just one week, he'd traversed the entire refuge, 220 air miles in all, negotiating thawing tundra and nearly a dozen stream crossings, his push driven by the urge to find food, a mate, and vacant territory.

10

Muskox on the Sagavanirktok

On a tundra plateau just east of the Sagavanirktok (Sag) River, an Arctic fox sprinted for safety, a golden plover piped out a warning, and ground squirrels dove for cover. High overhead, a gyrfalcon circled, keeping watch on its nest on a nearby cliff. The news was shared: a roving hunter had arrived.

The Wanderer reached the plateau on June 18, the tundra around him not yet greening up under the continuous sunlight. He picked up his pace when he detected the faint scent of caribou. Other than a few voles, a ptarmigan, and hatchlings plucked from a shorebird's nest, he'd eaten little for days, and a gnawing hunger kept him restless, moving. The scent strengthened as he moved west, yet he slowed and stopped at the top of a rise, well short of finding his prey.

He stopped to listen, not to the calls of Lapland longspurs and red-throated loons, but to the sounds of diesel trucks thundering down the Dalton Highway on the far side of the river. Perhaps he even heard the roar of machinery operating to the north. If it were dark at night, the northern horizon, less than a day's lope away, would glow with the lights of the sprawling Prudhoe Bay and Badami oil fields. What the wolf could sense, or comprehend, is unknowable, but his westward journey had come to an abrupt end.

Since the very onset of its existence, the pipeline corridor has been an uncertain place for wolves. Pipeline workers illegally fed some; others killed a few. Latter-day travelers have done the same. Prohibitions against the use of firearms in the corridor are often ignored when it comes to wolves. One year, just north of the side road to the village of Wiseman, wolves inexplicably denned within a quarter mile of the Dalton. Weeks-old pups soon wandered onto the road. By late summer, the entire litter had been flattened by vehicles.

Since leaving the refuge, the Wanderer had been crossing terrain explored and, in places, altered by oil companies. Traces of winter oil exploration were widespread, but the effort lies dormant in summer. Although his natal territory in Yukon-Charley was now well over four hundred air miles to the southeast, he carried with him ingrained and learned behaviors. Just as he'd shied away from the tractor trails and mining claims on the Seventymile River, he now turned away from the distant road. Perhaps the taint of diesel was all the warning he needed.

The plateau was in one of the two prime calving areas of the Central Arctic Caribou Herd. As the name implies, the herd roams the central portion of Arctic Alaska; calving takes place across a broad swath of the coastal plain from the Canning River west to the Colville River and is concentrated on either side of Prudhoe Bay. Soon after calving season, they disperse east and west to their summer range, the coastal breezes providing much-needed relief from insects. Due to late snowmelt on the coast, part of the Central Arctic Herd had already moved into the foothills of the Brooks Range, but as the weather warmed, the snow melted, and the tundra greened up, they straggled back north.

In autumn, much of the herd migrates south through the mountains to spend the winter on the south slope. Summer and winter ranges are only about 120 miles apart, but a small portion of the herd remains north of the mountains throughout the year, foraging on lichens exposed on wind-scoured ridges and tundra benches.

This year females led their calves into the uplands in search of new plant growth earlier than usual and into areas somewhat more populated with wolves and bears. Due to climate change, the coastal plain now gets more snow than in the past, which in turn delays the green-up. The change has wrought notable fluctuations in Arctic plant and animal communities, and on the people that rely on them.

When the Wanderer arrived on the terraces above the Sagavanirktok River in spring 2011, the Central Arctic Herd was in gradual decline, eventually dropping over the next five years from sixty-eight thousand to twenty-three thousand. Predation and disease did not appear to cause the decline, nor did ongoing development in the oil fields. Studies show that pregnant cows avoid active, industrial areas but since the herd had grown during peak oil development, biologists didn't believe it to be responsible. On the other hand, no one can say for certain how big the Central Arctic Herd might have grown without the loss of habitat and calving grounds to the oil fields.

The most important factor influencing the size of Arctic caribou herds is the survival of adult females. A survival rate of at least 84 percent indicates the herd is stable or possibly increasing, but during the herd's decline, female survival rates fell below 80 percent. Lingering cold and delayed snowmelt in consecutive years apparently contributed to high adult and yearling mortality. Spring migration is taxing on pregnant cows, and an extra month of winter reduces access to forage during a critical time. No other major weather events—such as the severe icing events that killed large numbers of the Western Arctic Herd—have been linked to the decline.

Looking back, researchers have since decided that two major factors accounted for the decline: high adult female mortality and animals switching herds. A portion of the Central Arctic Herd's range overlaps with that of the much larger Porcupine Herd. From 2013 to 2015, extensive mingling occurred between the two as the Porcupine Herd expanded its range, swamping the smaller herd. During the decline, large numbers of females switched herds and joined the larger herd when they occupied the same area. Generally, caribou follow the animals around them, in both the short term and long term. Nonetheless, as calving season approached, many of the "switchers" returned to their traditional grounds. Switching does not appear to be the primary factor that drove the reduction of the Central Arctic Herd, but rather overtaxed forage from the combined herds contributed to increased mortality. A few people still blame oil development for the decline, however, and some hunters blame predators and call for expanded wolf control.

THE WANDERER'S ODDS OF MAKING a kill on this slice of tundra, where competition was almost nonexistent, should have improved. Yet success continued to elude the young wolf. The scattered caribou on the terraces were not abundant, and on open, exposed tundra, it was hard to catch wary and fleet prey.

In his search for food, he trotted south into the uplands between the 180-mile-long Sagavanirktok ("strong current" in Iñupiaq) and Ivishak ("red river" or "red paint") Rivers. On the coast, the temperature was 36°F, the wind out of the northeast at fifteen miles per hour. Just inland as he passed by Franklin Bluffs, the skies were clear, it was 50°F, and a few mosquitoes were noticeable but not yet bothersome. Caribou were scarce and the few present shied away at his distant approach. Two bull muskox seemed unconcerned by his passage.

The multicolored Franklin Bluffs lining the east bank of the Sagavanirktok were named for Sir John Franklin, a British explorer who mapped the Arctic coastline in search of the Northwest Passage. On his third Arctic expedition in 1826, he reached and named Prudhoe Bay. Franklin and the 128 men of his two vessels, HMS *Terror* and HMS *Erebus*, were last seen alive in Canada's eastern Arctic in 1845. In 2014, a Canadian search team located the wreck of the *Erebus* in the eastern Arctic. Two years later they found the *Terror* some distance from where the ships had been trapped and crushed in the ice.

The Wanderer was unaware that he was in a race against time to find and catch calves while they were still young and vulnerable. The peak of calving had passed. Many were now already strong and fast enough to outrun a wolf. Some were still at risk, but their odds of survival increased almost daily. If only the Wanderer could find a large herd, he'd have plenty to eat. A young calf would provide him with little more than five to eight pounds of lean meat, but several would sustain him.

Because they also die from accidents and disease, large herds often leave dead calves in their wake. In Sunset Pass, a photographer once watched a dozen cows with calves approach and cross a shallow stream. The adults crossed with ease, but the calves struggled in the slight current over the cobblestones. On the far bank, one faltered, its leg broken in the rocks. Despite the mother's frantic urgings, it was unable to go on. After she left, the injured calf lay in the tussocks awaiting its fate. Later that afternoon, a dark gray wolf killed it, flayed it open, and devoured the choice organs, leaving the rest to the jaegers and foxes. The wolf put a quick end to what otherwise would have been prolonged suffering. The photographer recalled that early naturalists believed that wolves deliberately drove caribou into the rocks in order to break their legs.

The Wanderer had not killed an adult caribou in many days. He'd assuaged his hunger with small prey and likely some carrion. But here on the tundra terraces just south of Franklin Bluffs was his first encounter with muskox; the short, blocky, brown-and-cream-colored animal would feed him for days if only he could figure out how to bring one down.

When compared to other large Alaskan mammals, a muskox is an almost otherworldly looking beast. At a distance, a solitary muskox can be mistaken for a bear. The Iñupiat call them *itomingmak*, "the animal with skin like a beard," referring to the long, coarse guard hairs that trail to the ground. Under the outer coat is a luxurious, soft brown undercoat called *qiviuq* or *qiviut*, often said to be the rarest fiber in the world, softer than cashmere, warmer than wool. Mature bulls stand about five feet tall at the shoulder and weigh up to eight hundred pounds; cows are a third smaller. In spring, cows give birth to single calves that weigh about twenty-five pounds and grow rapidly. Muskox are both browsers and grazers; because they are poorly adapted for digging through heavy snow for food, their winter range is generally restricted to areas with low snowfall or those blown free of snow. They are true high-Arctic animals and often share winter range with caribou.

At the close of the last ice age, muskox were distributed across northern Europe, Asia, Greenland, Canada, and Alaska but disappeared from Europe and Asia by the mid-1800s and from Alaska in the 1920s. By then, the only remaining animals lived in East Greenland and Arctic Canada.

Although their extinction in Alaska is commonly thought to have been due to the introduction of firearms or commercial whalers hunting for meat or hides, most scholars agree that muskox were extremely rare in northern Alaska prior to the arrival of Europeans and the proliferation of firearms. Iñupiat hunters, facing famine, apparently killed off the last muskox in northwestern Alaska.

In 1930, thirty-four were captured in East Greenland and eventually transplanted to Nunivak Island in the Bering Sea. The animals thrived there and served as the reservoir for reintroductions to other parts of Alaska, including to the Arctic National Wildlife Refuge in 1969. A dozen more were released on the Kavik River. Muskox numbers east of the Canning River peaked in 1995 at 700, declining to fewer than 250 by 2011. A number of factors, including bear predation and starvation due to weather and food availability, contributed to the decline.

Both male and female muskox have horns, but a bull's are larger and heavier, with broad bases that span nearly the entire forehead. A bull's skull is fortified with four inches of horn and three inches of bone to protect the brain during fall rutting jousts, when the bulls battle in violent headbutting contests. After a period of stylized challenge displays, two bulls charge at top speed from distances of up to fifty yards and collide headfirst. They then back away, swinging their heads from side to side. The jolting conflict continues until one bull capitulates and runs off. The muskox derives its name from the strong musky odor the bulls emit during the rut to attract females.

Above all else, muskox are known for their circle defense against predators. When threatened, they rush together and draw a tight circle, calves next to their mothers or huddled inside the circle, the adults all facing outward, a phalanx of heads and horns. Adults, especially mature bulls, are dangerous. Sometimes, a bull will charge from the circle and scatter a menacing wolf pack, then quickly rejoin the circle.

If the herd stays together and doesn't panic, the defensive formation is highly effective. When a pack attacks a band of muskox, the whole thrust of an assault is to confuse and panic the herd, then isolate a calf. A young muskox caught away from the herd is much easier for a pack to chase down and kill. But while the circle defense works well against wolves, it's less effective against experienced grizzlies that attack head-on and overpower their prey.

Calves are always prime targets for wolves, and just now many cows were trailed by young calves, the perfect size and weight for the Wanderer to kill, but he was inexperienced and wary, having never encountered muskox before. And lone wolves seldom break a circle defense. Big animals that clustered together and stood their ground were beyond his experience and seemed somehow menacing. More than once, he was charged by a bull, but he dodged those lethal horns with ease. A show of aggression from a bull or cow was enough to rebuff his tentative challenge. Nonetheless, he approached every muskox he found and then, after a cursory test for vulnerability, continued on his way south.

On June 19, the Wanderer trotted into the foothills between the Ivishak and Sag Rivers, ten miles southeast of the old Happy Valley pipeline construction camp on the Dalton Highway. Small herds of caribou grazed the surrounding slopes. Broods of rock ptarmigan meandered through the willow thickets; horned larks flushed from the tussocks. Once again, the wolf was leaving the flat tundra for more familiar alpine terrain, rapidly greening up.

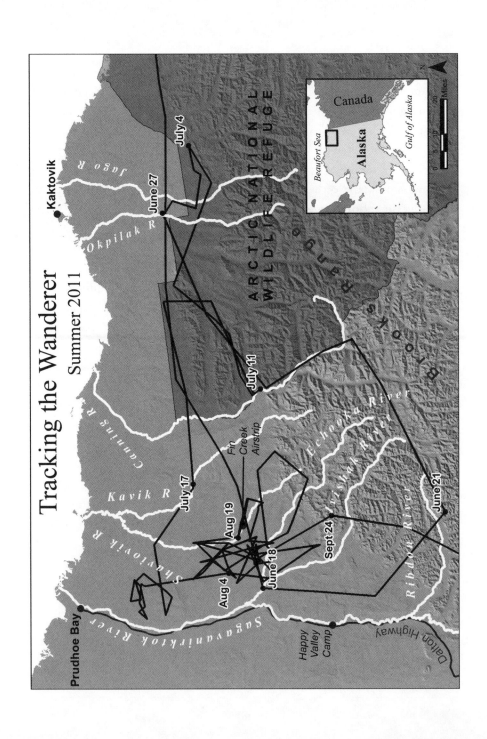

11

The Summer Solstice Loop

By the summer solstice, the Wanderer had moved forty-four air miles southeast to the vaulting mountains in the upper Ribdon River valley, home to an active wolf pack. Recent killing winters with deep snow had contributed to a sharp decline in the local Dall sheep population; most gathered in the headwaters rather than farther down the valley. Like elsewhere in the northern mountains, sheep forage was never abundant. Small bands of ewes, with month-old lambs in tow, grazed the south-facing slopes, but due to terrain and the ever-vigilant ewes, the lambs would not be easy to catch.

The next day the Wanderer traversed another forty air miles through the heart of the Philip Smith Mountains and descended to the Marsh Fork of the Canning River, in the Arctic refuge. This, too, was Dall sheep country. Already the slopes were green and the river lined with blooming dwarf fireweed, arctic milkvetch, and wild sweetpea. In these warmer mountains, the mosquitoes had hatched and tormented the wolf whenever the winds abated.

The Marsh Fork is a popular summer wilderness-rafting stream. The first river runners were already on the river, enjoying a moderately difficult trip with shallow segments and some Class III whitewater. Many floaters, some wearing head nets, usually hike away from the river for the chance to see varied wildlife—sheep, muskox, and perhaps wolves.

The following day, fifteen air miles to the northeast, the Wanderer crossed a 3,300-foot windswept basin amid a jumble of 6,000-foot peaks. He then crested a 4,600-foot ridge and dropped down to the upper Canning River, the rugged character of the terrain slowing his movements. Blackish crustose lichen covered the rocks and, when wet, turned slick and dangerous. He injured a paw traversing a steep slope but kept going. Brooks Range marmots, only a few weeks out of hibernation, whistled out warnings, then ducked beneath the rocks.

As he negotiated narrow alpine trails carved out by sheep, the wolf brushed against outcrops of marine invertebrate and coral fossils, an indelible record of the earth's violent transformation. He limped along over fossilized segments of age-old trilobites.

Descending the refulgent slopes of the Canning, the Wanderer, escorted by swarming mosquitoes, crossed alpine tundra alive with flowering mountain avens, moss campion, white heather, and Arctic lupine. Soft summer sunshine sparked green fire across the hillsides. On the river bottom, willow thickets harbored ptarmigan and squirrels, and ever more biting insects. The Canning, the longest river in the Arctic refuge, begins amid jagged limestone peaks and flows north across the west end of three subranges of the Brooks Range: the Third Range, the Shublik Mountains, and the Sadlerochit Mountains. From the upper river, he proceeded downstream thirty-one miles north to its confluence with Cache Creek on the south perimeter of the Third Range. Then, on June 25, the Wanderer's journey took a circuitous turn. Why he turned east here is unknown, but perhaps the scent of roving caribou lured him in that direction.

The Wanderer abandoned the river bottoms and rambled northeast thirty air miles in one day, to Fire Creek, a tributary of the Sadlerochit

River on the north side of the Sadlerochit Mountains. The next day he skirted the mountains, swam or waded both the Sadlerochit and Hula-hula Rivers, and emerged thirty-three air miles from the mountains onto the flat, soggy coastal plain, where scattered caribou grazed the now fast-greening tundra.

The Wanderer traversed this immense landscape by negotiating decades-old trails and passes used by migrating herds. Yet they eluded him, as he found only small, scattered bands. Desperate for food, he likely made several clumsy charges, panicking the potential prey to take flight. When bigger groups splinter apart, some animals lose sight of their attacker, giving the predator the advantage.

Finally, on June 27, after a jolting chase through tussock flats, the Wanderer brought down an adult caribou in a tundra marsh on the east bank of the Okpilak River. In his typical fashion, he ripped open the paunch and yanked out and devoured the liver, spleen, kidneys, and heart, all rich in minerals and vitamins. Only after ravenously gulping down the choice organs and fatty tissue did he tear into the muscle protein, lapping the rich blood as he fed. The feast broke a long famine and came just as he was getting desperate.

The Wanderer spent the next three days gorging on the much-needed protein. The weather was cloudy and cooler on the plain than in the mountains, in the low forties, the wind light and variable to ten miles per hour, which held the mosquitoes at bay and gave him a chance to eat and fully rest.

Looking back on the Wanderer's journey, wolf biologist Mathew Sorum remarked, "What was fascinating to that date was how rarely kills had occurred. [He] must have been eating small game, birds. But that's what wolves do. Wolves possess an extraordinary ability to forego food for long periods of time, from ten days to two weeks, or perhaps even longer, with minimal loss of function. Recovery from fasting is swift."

Next, the Wanderer continued east four miles to a 1,100-foot hill just shy of the Jago River with an unrestricted view of the surrounding tundra.

Most years, the Jago plain would be alive with caribou, but this time it was still vacant. After pausing on the hilltop, the wolf turned due south into the foothills between the Jago and Okpilak Rivers, then moved eastward to the point where the Aichilik River emerged from the mountains, arriving on the Fourth of July.

From the bank of the Aichilik, the wolf promptly turned around and headed back west, sticking to the mountain slopes. His circuitous trek took him back to the Sadlerochit Mountains and through Sunset Pass to Itkil-yariak Creek, not far from where he'd first crossed eleven days earlier. Most of the snow had melted, and grasses and sedges were now thrust into the light. A few caribou, likely members of the Central Arctic Herd, grazed leisurely in the distance. The mosquitoes grew ever more numerous.

Spending less than a day on the north side of the mountains, the Wanderer made a U-turn to retrace his steps back through Sunset Pass, ending that day's twenty-mile jaunt at the head of the Sadlerochit River. He then coursed the highlands and dropped back down to Cache Creek. On July 11, he was back at the upper Canning River, the same spot he'd been on June 25. In less than two and a half weeks, the wolf had traversed over two hundred miles of rugged terrain, averaging nearly fifteen miles per travel day. GPS collars record only point-to-point measurements, so his loop may have covered many more miles than that.

What drove the wolf on this long loop? Was it solely hunger? The quest for a mate? An exploration of new country or of territory to claim as his own? He'd coursed treeless tundra and mountains stark and bare. He'd trespassed the territory of at least one wolf pack, maybe others, but there was no way to know whether he'd made contact or, if he did, how he avoided conflict. Most probably, his was not an exploratory lark but true appetitive behavior—a searching and craving that could only be appeased by fulfillment. Killing and consuming prey was likely the whole point of this journey.

The wolf began and ended his foray across from a tundra patch in the middle of the Canning River that was oddly designated Shublik Island.

Anywhere else in Alaska it would be called a willow bar, a typical sand-and-cobble aggregate covered with grass and shrubs in a braided river. A century before, explorer E. K. Leffingwell visited the island and the huts of a traditional Iñupiat hunting camp. The people were hunting caribou and fishing through the ice for Arctic char and grayling. Leffingwell noted the Iñupiat's long association with the wolf, an animal they call *Amaguq*.

The late Bob Stephenson, an ADF&G wolf researcher, held an uncommon respect for Alaska Native knowledge, especially that of the Nunamiut, the inland Iñupiat, of Anaktuvuk Pass. He collected natural history information as well as cultural practices. On the coast, the Wolf Dance, part of a revival of Kivgiq, the Messenger Feast, tells a traditional story of swallows turning into wolves. The dancing throughout the Messenger Feast represents the animals that were the first to learn how to sing and dance and were transformed into human form by the Eagle Mother. In the Wolf Dance, dancers wear a wolf-tail belt and a wolf-nose headband decorated with colored beads on a caribou-skin backing. By displaying the unique features of the wolf—the pointed ears, the long snout, the brushy tail—the headband and belt symbolize the significance of wolf fur in the context of successful hunting practices. Hunting them requires great tracking skill and ingenuity, and they are primarily acquired for their prized fur. In the past, only a person who killed a wolf could wear its fur, a sign of a particular talent for hunting them. Wearing a wolf's tail in a ceremonial context carried multiple meanings. Like an amulet, the fur not only honored the wolf's *Inua* ("spirit") but bestowed the wearer with special wolf-like powers, such as speed, endurance, and strength.

In the not-too-distant past, some men wore the fur of wolf heads for parka hoods, a recognition of them as hunters endowed with certain wolf-like qualities. Because they were such highly valued and special animals in Iñupiat culture, the hunting of wolves, and the use of their fur, was governed by taboos and rituals.

Now, as then, many Iñupiat people move inland to the foothills in winter, where they fish, trap, and hunt for caribou and sometimes wolves.

Other people hunt here too, but for more than caribou. The island and mountain range take their name from the Shublik Formation, a Triassic uplift with abundant marine vertebrate and invertebrate fossils. The fractured Shublik Formation and the underlying Ivishak sandstone draw the interest of petroleum engineers who see the opportunity for shale-oil extraction via fracking, which carries enormous implications for Alaska.

The Wanderer's two-hundred-mile loop not only covered new ground and ultimately provided him with food but also took him from late spring into true Arctic summer, a time fraught with its own unique perils. For all life on the North Slope, the next few weeks would prove challenging.

12

Mosquitoes and Endless Daylight

A dense, opaque cloud of mosquitoes swarmed around the twitching wolf lying prone on the damp tundra as he tried to stay cool in the 70°F heat. Thickets of insects ringed his eyes, peppered his snout and face, and clustered on his inner legs and underbelly. An incessant drone filled the air around him. His thin, blotchy summer coat, shed of its long winter guard hairs, offered feckless protection from the insatiable blood-sucking horde. His eyes blinked constantly; his ears twitched spasmodically. Every few seconds he'd shake his head, rake his face with a paw, or snap at the air. Smears of blood stained his muzzle, belly, and thighs. Without wind, there was no respite from the torment.

Each day throughout the Wanderer's two-hundred-mile loop, the mosquitoes had increased; then one warm day the entire tundra seemed to hatch, insects exploding into the air. Their assaults on the wolf, and every other living animal, blossomed overnight from bothersome to fearsome. Almost every caribou on the Arctic plain pushed closer to the coast, seeking relief along the windswept shores of the Beaufort Sea. Some of them waded into the shallows; others stood on cooling shelf ice. Bears, wolverines, and foxes found respite as best they could; squirrels went underground. Many birds simply feasted on the insects.

In a burrow in a small pingo a short distance from where the Wanderer thrashed, a female Arctic fox huddled in the cool air until her pups' demand for food pushed her out into the swarms, where her mate already sought prey. Rodent populations were rather limited near the den, and both adults coursed far and wide to gather enough voles, brown lemmings, and bird eggs to satiate them. Although brown lemmings were scarce this year, their populations periodically explode, reaching peak abundance every three to five years. In these peak years, weasels, foxes, and snowy owls live and prosper on the surfeit. Owl nesting zooms upward when brown lemmings are abundant and crashes when they disappear. An abrupt decrease in their numbers is not attributable to hordes flinging themselves off cliffs and into the sea, as depicted in staged documentaries. Rather, a combination of weather, predation, food quantity and quality, and genetic changes in the population causes these wide fluctuations. Also contrary to folktales, lemmings do not migrate, although some may move into marginal habitat during population peaks.

A related small rodent, the collared lemming, is also sought by foxes, owls, and wolves. Although not classified as a true lemming by scientists, it is the only true rodent that turns white in winter. In most Arctic regions, collared lemmings are never as abundant as brown lemmings. Both species were less than abundant just now, and the foxes, as well as the Wanderer, hunted hard, trying to find a few to eat.

The postcalving caribou aggregations had begun to fragment, with some moving south into the mountains, stirrings of a long gradual move to the wintering grounds. Insect harassment and the search for better pasture drove them into the windy ridges. Roving wolves followed the dispersing herds but enjoyed limited success. The maturing calves were now strong, fast, and able to elude wolves and bears alike. Researchers estimate that wolves are successful only in one in ten hunts, with a vastly higher success ratio when young calves are the prey. The window of easy prey had come to an end.

Many of the insect-harried wolves, like the Wanderer, then turned to alternate prey. But that bounty also would soon thin out. For nesting birds, time is precious: a brief span to court, then shelter nests, eggs, and young, with many species beginning their migration south in early August. After the waterfowl nests empty and the fledglings take wing, predators again face lean times. The spring feast lasts only days, and this year in the core calving area, almost none at all. Prey on the arctic prairies can be so scarce that even snowy owls migrate in search of food, sometimes settling in winter on the frozen Bering Sea ice, where they subsist on eiders overwintering in the polynyas.

AFTER RESTING A DAY in a willow thicket at the confluence of Cache Creek with the Canning River, the Wanderer retraced his steps east and two days later again traversed Sunset Pass to reach Marsh Creek, a site he'd visited exactly a month before. Once more, he passed through a pack's territory undetected and unscathed. The mosquitoes gave him no respite, though, and despite having already moved fifty miles in two days, he pushed on. Like other Arctic animals sorely tested by the insect plague, the wolf's eyes looked painted on, lacking the light of his typical venatic zeal.

He didn't go far; the next day he traveled just a mile north to a mercifully windswept bluff on the east bank of Marsh Creek. From his perch, the Wanderer commanded a view of the creek's twenty-mile meander across the tussock flats to Camden Bay, where in most years caribou gathered in the cooling onshore wind.

On July 16, the wolf trudged twenty-seven miles west across the soggy tundra to wade Tamayariak Creek, near where he'd crossed weeks earlier. The next day saw another twenty-five-mile jaunt to a wide, braided gravel bar on the eighty-mile-long Kavik River, twelve miles outside the eastern boundary of the Arctic refuge.

Although the Kavik is a rather minor watercourse, the name is familiar to many people. Walt Morey's 1968 novel, *Kävik the Wolf Dog*, won the Dutton Animal Book Award and popularized the name for young readers. A short distance upstream from the Wanderer's location sits the original West Kavik oil exploration camp, the start of a tractor trail leading southwest a dozen miles to drilling test holes in the foothills. The site now known as the Kavik River Camp, advertised as the "farthest north bed and breakfast," hosts researchers, hikers, birders, and hunters. National Geographic's reality show *Life Below Zero* featured Susan Aikens, the camp's proprietor.

Portions of the Kavik drainage serve as winter habitat for a few moose and muskox, but it was dangerous terrain for a wolf. Caribou hunting season had just opened, and many hunters would not hesitate to shoot a wolf. Dispersing wolves are particularly vulnerable, as they travel through unfamiliar terrain and are unaccustomed to the human activity there. In spring 1991, on the Canning River, an Iñupiat hunter shot a dispersing female from Denali National Park's Headquarters Pack, its territory of origin located 435 air miles to the south.

For two days the Wanderer lingered in the willow thickets downstream from the Kavik camp. Either he had killed a small caribou or found a caribou gut pile. In the shelter of the willows, the mosquitoes were horrendous but his hunger insatiable. He gorged on the scraps and rested nearby, apparently undetected by hunters if any were about.

After regaining his strength, the Wanderer moved north twenty miles to the Shaviovik River wetlands, an extensive waterfowl nesting area. Large numbers of Pacific and red-throated loons, geese, swans, and shorebirds nest and rear their broods in the ponds and marshes. It was almost 50°F on the coast, clear and very windy, which kept the insect horde at bay. Caribou were scattered across the marsh and surrounding tundra too, feeding placidly on the abundant sedges and cottongrass.

Just to the west, in the terraces north of Franklin Bluffs, the wolf settled down on a relatively dry tundra plateau, bordered on the west by the Sag River and on the east by the Kadleroshilik River. Wetlands bounded the north and south end of this tapering eight-hundred-foot tableland. Over the next two weeks, he never crossed the Sag, got no closer to the Dalton Highway than 2.5 miles, and stayed a dozen miles south of Deadhorse, gateway to the massive oil fields. The Wanderer did not even venture out onto the sprawling Sag River delta, with its pingos, polygons, and pothole ponds, but seemed content to stay on the 160-square-mile plateau. He'd found caribou.

Was it simply a pocket of accessible prey that ended the wolf's constant travel? Or something else? Arctic summer had peaked, with mosquitoes at their worst, and this windswept tundra plateau offered prolonged respite from the torment. Wolves possess an ingrained ability to recognize promising country, to somehow determine a sustainable amount of prey. Could the Wanderer have sensed something about this particular location? Could he have recognized a vacant and productive territory to claim for his own? Ever since biologist John Burch had collared the Wanderer, he'd been diligently satellite tracking him. He speculated that besides finding a concentration of prey and a reprieve from insects, the Wanderer may have found a partner. Had the young male been anywhere close to the Yukon-Charley Rivers Preserve, a routine overflight and visual check could have resolved the issue. As it was, the Wanderer was in the land of the hyperboreans, a several-hours-long, often risky flight away from his territory of origin. His status remained a mystery.

The sociability of wolves is all about reproduction and survival. They need each other. Given the size and power of their prey, they are much more successful when hunting in a group. And as a member of a pack, a wolf's odds for survival, especially in winter, are higher. Roaming alone through vast regions of hostile, unfamiliar country, a true tabula rasa, exacts not only a physical strain but an unknowable mental strain as well. If, in fact, the Wanderer had connected with another wolf, the linkup must have generated both excitement and intense relief.

As the Wanderer's roaming demonstrates, long-distance travel is normal for wolves. Subordinate wolves regularly course their home territory alone in search of food, sometimes for weeks at a time, before eventually returning to the pack, only to leave again. This pattern continues until one day they make a permanent break from their natal territory. Given the vast wilderness and distances involved, the hazards of such journeys, and their relative scarcity on the Arctic coast, it is rather astonishing that two could join up in that far distant place.

Very little is known about how two lone wolves team up and bond. Is it solely by chance or through specific actions? Unlike moose, caribou, and elk, which come together in breeding season with extravagant, often noisy displays, dispersing wolves link up quietly, outside the breeding season, well before the period of mating receptivity. Perhaps dispersers meet in vacant territory in the same way they primarily hunt: by scent. A wolf lives in a world of scent that swirls and drifts on every current of air and clings to the ground and brush, rocks and soil, imparting information beyond human understanding. Scent informs every action a wolf takes and guides every decision. A mere trace may carry all the clues a wolf needs to determine the status of the maker. A splash of urine may be sufficient for identification. Or perhaps dispersers meet by tracking, or through chance encounters while hunting; a lone wolf is almost always hungry and hunting. Since a disperser is essentially hunting a mate, initial contact may result when the two hunters cross paths or scent trails.

Wolf song is integral to their communication, and messages are sent over long distances. They howl for a variety of reasons. One reason is to advertise their presence and avoid unnecessary, perhaps even lethal, encounters with neighbors. Much howling is a spacing message: "Stay away. Keep your distance." Another is to draw a scattered pack or pups together. Wolf song can convey motion, location, fear, apprehension, and much more; the entirety of the information that wolves exchange through howling will never be known to us. Occasionally a wolf in one pack will answer the howling of another pack, but not always. Sometimes a howl can serve as a homing beacon, but with dangerous consequences. Perhaps a disperser's howl carries a unique signal, but because it must also keep a relatively low profile, it rarely scent marks or howls. Instead, it slips silently away from occupied territory. To date, the Wanderer had proven adept at avoiding lethal encounters with other wolves, as well as humans.

How dispersers sometimes gain acceptance into a new pack is mostly conjecture. Contact between unrelated wolves can turn lethal—especially dangerous for a lone wolf. But if the death of the breeding male or female, or both, disrupts the social order of the resident pack, then a dispersing wolf may be readily accepted into a new pack rather than attacked. Clearly, the loss of a breeding adult destabilizes a pack, often causing it to break up into smaller packs and alter their hunting territory. The Wanderer may have encountered a small pack led by a female accompanied by her offspring and been adopted as the future breeding male. Or, more likely, given the few wolves on the Arctic plain, the Wanderer paired with a lone female. Two lone wolves would not automatically fight; it is easier to kill another wolf when it's outnumbered. If for no other reason than to improve their chances when hunting, two lone wolves may be open to pairing.

The Wanderer was now three years old and had yet to breed. In an established pack, the dominant male and female normally restrict and control breeding. It once was believed that most dispersers were young females reaching their sexual maturity, the drive to mate pushing them from the pack. In theory, they couldn't wait for the older, dominant females to die before they had a chance to mate. Current research, however, indicates that younger females sometimes breed with the dominant male and that young males disperse at a higher rate than previously thought.

The initial bonding exchange between two dispersers has rarely, if ever, been witnessed in the wild. But from observations of the body language of both captive and wild wolves, we can speculate. If, in fact, the Wanderer did find a mate, it may have happened this way:

Late July on the plateau remained dry and windy, with several periods of dense fog drifting in on the northeast wind. Small bands of caribou meandered the tundra, grazing on the abundant sedges and cottongrass and resting in the stout breeze. Two lone wolves, a male and a female, hunting the same draws and thickets, eventually alerted to one another by scent. At some point they saw each other and stopped to calculate risk. They made sounds that each recognized as nonaggressive. Tentatively they approached, each taking on different body postures: The Wanderer at first held his tail high but quickly lowered it, signifying he was not aggressive. Ears forward, head and chest up, tail freely wagging, he approached the female, who was wary of the bigger, stronger male. Her posture signaled a guarded submission. She advanced in a crouch, tail down, mouth closed, ears drawn flat. Her scent gave no hint of relatedness.

After tentative sniffing and smelling, the two brushed against each another, rubbed cheeks, and licked faces. The Wanderer then laid his head across the female's back. She bounced away with snarls and bared teeth. They came together again, and she rolled on her back and exposed her underside, almost whimpering. Over and over, they went through a full range of acceptance displays only to break apart in playful leaps and short chases. A few times, both wolves bared their teeth, but they did not fight. These behaviors lasted for hours, perhaps for days, until a firm link was established. Once the pair began to hunt, share prey, travel together, and defend their new territory, their bond was complete. The following spring, they would breed, their quest fulfilled.

DISPERSERS THAT COUPLE IN JULY have months together before the female comes into heat the following winter, between late February and mid-March. Wolves are said to mate for life, demonstrating a strong, long-lasting bond. Older breeders, with their broader life experience and possession of an established territory, are thought to be more successful. But those pairing in a new territory, of which they possess limited knowledge, face several basic challenges. First, they must hunt successfully together and defend their claim. Both must survive the lean autumn and winter months. Then, they must breed and have pups. And finally, they must hunt well enough to feed and raise their young. Any new pairing appears rather tenuous, without a guaranteed outcome.

The tundra plateau, where the Wanderer now lingered, was not big enough to serve as territory year-round, but it held certain advantages. Competition or threat from other wolves was negligible. A limited number of caribou and muskox would be available even in winter. But was there enough sustenance for two wolves to survive the winter? A big drawback was the lack of suitable terrain for denning. That would have to take place in the mountains, where other packs held sway. The Wanderer had already traversed other areas that supported adequate year-round prey but had not settled in, likely due to the presence of the established packs. If indeed the Wanderer had found a partner and was staking claim to territory, further exploration of a broader area would be necessary to determine its suitability.

In the fifteen days the Wanderer stayed on the plateau, he traveled a measurable distance of just fifty-nine air miles, an average of about four miles per day, with the longest move barely nine miles. Maybe he hadn't joined up with another wolf, but he'd certainly found good hunting terrain. The plateau was wide open, with little ground cover. In such terrain, caribou could easily spot a predator at a distance and move off, and the wolf had lost his speed advantage over the calves, which now possessed surprising stamina. Yet the plateau was riven with numerous small drainages, and their folds offered cover and concealment for a stalking wolf. Although wolves are coursing hunters, they are fluent at reading terrain, and this ability gave the Wanderer some advantage.

A wolf's stalk is straightforward: normally a slow, steady walk toward the prey, little or no creeping like a lynx or a fox, followed by an all-out chase. Ground features on the plateau would allow him to get close before breaking into a sprint. Even so, not every chase was successful; most ended up scattering the small groups and driving them off. The Wanderer challenged every caribou he encountered in order to detect vulnerability. A wolf's senses are supremely attuned to prey behaviors and subtle signs that indicate weakness. If the Wanderer gained no clear advantage in a pursuit, or discovered no frailty, he'd break off and try another caribou. For the first time since leaving Ivvavik, he was making regular kills, likely late-born calves. If in fact the Wanderer had paired up, his increased hunting success may have been attributable to cooperative effort.

Another factor may have slowed the Wanderer's movements somewhat. July is the warmest month on the North Slope, with temperatures rising into the eighties in the foothills. On the plateau that summer, July 28 was the hottest day, with a high of 72°F. (The low that day was 38°F.) While it was often foggy and damp, there had been no precipitation that entire month, and as it waned, the caribou began to move away as the temperatures peaked and the winds died down, making the insects intolerable. Some went toward the coast, others south into the foothills.

As July drew to a close, prey was thinning out and getting harder to catch. The plateau may have offered terrain advantages for a hunting wolf, or pair of wolves, but stress on forage and insect harassment scattered the earlier concentration of caribou. The Wanderer began to broaden his search and expand his territory.

In early August, just as the insect plague began to waver slightly, the situation on the plateau further eroded with the first stirrings of early migration. In August of most years, the Central Arctic Herd begins to move slowly and irregularly southward to higher elevations. The migration is oriented principally north-south, extending from the summer range and calving grounds on the coastal plain to their winter range in the mountains and foothills of the Brooks Range. Early on, their movements are almost undetectable, but autumn's initial severe storm triggers a general shift toward their winter habitat. These annual migrations, often between tundra and taiga, are a necessity because even caribou may not survive year-round in the Arctic. When the first deadly winter winds come to the tundra, packing the snow into concrete-hard drifts and sealing the forage below, most caribou are already well on their way to the wintering grounds, where the wind shears the forage clear of snow and the protective timber keeps the snow loose and easy to shovel aside for feeding.

Far to the east, the Porcupine Herd was already moving south, and by August 10, few would be left in the mountains, the majority roving even farther east into Yukon Territory. It wouldn't be until September that they would begin to circle back west into Alaska and populate the south slopes of the Brooks Range. With the majority of both herds wintering well to the south, wolves would struggle to survive on the coastal plain.

On August 2, the sun set on the Arctic coast for the first time in eighty-three days, a sign of the inexorable slide into the long, dark polar night. All over, millions of animals were on the move. Only a hardy few could survive the coming season without moving south. Two days later, under overcast and windy skies, the Wanderer, either alone or with his partner, abandoned the plateau and trotted due south twenty-five miles. He'd never see the plateau again.

13

In Grizzly Country

Instead of continuing south into the Brooks Range, the Wanderer stopped between the Shaviovik and Ivishak Rivers to hunt the tundra uplands, higher but similar to the terrain he'd recently vacated. August remained drier than usual and warm, around 50°F, averaging a significant 3.4°F above normal. The dwindling mosquitoes continued their ferocious assault until the first frost on the 18th. Frequent winds off the foothills provided relief both for the wolf and the local caribou, who were fattening for their push south through the range.

Daylight still persisted for nearly twenty hours, but each day was nearly fifteen minutes shorter than the previous, with the sun no longer high in the sky. On hazy days, sun dogs braced the sun, a harbinger of the coming cold. The tundra was tinted with the broad brush of autumnal colors, the slopes emblazoned with scarlet bearberry and the watercourse and ponds lined with golden willows. An ephemeral dusting of snow on the foothills conveyed a sense of urgency to the caribou foraging on the summer's fading plants.

Except for a two-day ramble into the foothills east of the old Happy Valley airstrip on the Dalton Highway, the Wanderer, and perhaps his companion, sortied back and forth across the tundra ridges. The locations gathered by his GPS tracking collar revealed no pattern to the roving except that he visited all points of the compass within an area of less than five hundred square miles. Perhaps the Wanderer had found a concentration of caribou, or competition may have influenced his movements. The grazing herd had likely attracted other wolves as well as bears.

Throughout his long journey, the Wanderer had crossed paths with several grizzly bears. He'd been reared in the Tanana Hills, home to both grizzlies and black bears. Since crossing the tree line on the south slope of the Brooks Range, he'd encountered only grizzlies, as black bears preferred the safety of timber. On the coastal plain he'd seen few bears. In most years he would have crossed paths with more; without the lure of abundant newborn calves, few grizzlies had ventured onto the plain. During the spring calving season, bears seem to be impacted by a variety of factors other than just the location of the herds. Annual variations in snowmelt, for example, influence their abundance and distribution. The late spring thaw in 2011 apparently kept many bears away from the plain and back in the mountains. The mountain grizzlies in most summers often hunt all the way to the edge of the sea ice.

The Wanderer shared these uplands with several grizzlies, then in hyperphagia—an intense period of feeding driven by a biological need to bulk up prior to denning. To survive hibernation, a bear must gorge itself to build layers of thick fat. Ripened berries are their major source of food. Wolves also eat a surprising amount of berries, especially when the hunting has been poor. Abundant blueberries likely lured the Wanderer into prime grizzly feeding zones. Squirrel colonies attracted both predators.

During berry season, wolves often become omnivores. Berries are wolves' primary source of food in many regions for a month or more. Research in Voyageurs National Park in Minnesota revealed that berries can make up to 83 percent of a pack's weekly diet during the berry season's peak. They turn to berries not because they prefer them over prey but because, as researchers described, berries are "starvation food." The ripening of abundant blueberries corresponds in Voyageurs and Alaska to a time when fawns and calves have matured and are no longer easy prey, before snow and cold shifts to favor wolves. Autumn is a lean time for wolves, so eating berries likely helps them minimize weight loss. Gorging on berries requires far fewer calories than searching a wide area and chasing after elusive prey. According to the research, wolves do not get as many calories from berries as they would from prey animals, but at least the berries partially appease their hunger; however, wolves eating predominantly berries are almost certainly losing weight. Studies of captive coyotes and foxes have shown that both species lose weight when fed a diet of fruit. Wolves are no different.

Arctic ground squirrels provide grizzlies with a fair amount of protein. In summer, bears move to the river bars and well-drained ridges to excavate squirrel colonies, but as autumn progresses, these large rodents become harder to find. In response to diminishing daylight, females retreat underground for up to eight months, considered the longest hibernation period on earth. The squirrels that linger aboveground through early October are almost always males; they hibernate as soon as they lay on enough body fat to survive the winter.

During hibernation, ground squirrels enter a state of torpor, their metabolic rates and body temperatures drastically lowered for up to three weeks at a time to conserve energy. Their body temperature drops from about 99°F to as low as 27°F, a condition referred to as supercooling and the lowest ever measured in a mammal. Between periods of torpor, they periodically rouse but, while still asleep, shiver for up to fifteen hours to raise their body temperature back to normal. The rewarming period usually lasts one to two days before they return to their previous state. This type of hibernation is rare among mammals, and scientists are still studying this unique physiological behavior. Males emerge from hibernation in spring having lost almost a third of their body weight, while females come out around two to three weeks later.

Grizzlies in hyperphagia may or may not be more aggressive than in summer, but certainly when food is scarce, they will vigorously defend what they find. Even though blueberries and, later, soapberries are important foods in fall, caribou gut piles left by hunters attract both bears and wolves, as well as smaller predators. In a world of scent, carrion doesn't stay undiscovered very long.

Ravens quickly find kills and carrion. Biologists often describe a symbiotic relationship between ravens and wolves. Some Native Americans call them "wolf birds." For example, if a raven locates a relatively intact carcass that they cannot tear open, they will begin to call loudly, attracting other ravens, which in turn draws in larger predators capable of flaying the carcass, providing a bounty for all. Both wolves and bears readily respond to the raucous calling of ravens.

Grizzlies are successful predators of newborn caribou. In one Denali National Park study, grizzlies killed 34 percent of all calves lost to predators within the first two weeks of life. Bear predation declined markedly as calves aged and matured. Researchers found it rare for a bear to kill one older than ten days. Wolf predation also spiked in the week after the peak of calving and then declined once calves reached about two weeks of age. Bears are also more likely to encounter and kill calves as calving density decreases, an indication that mass calving, the "calving spurt," is an effective antipredation strategy with respect to grizzlies. Wolves' hunting success in autumn is very low.

In the rare instance when a bear does kill an adult caribou, moose, or muskox, it will gorge, bury the carcass in dirt and vegetation, then lie on it or sleep nearby to protect it from competitors. If a grizzly makes a kill late in the season or takes over a largely intact carcass, it may stay with the remains until it has been consumed, long after the usual hibernation time in early October. Access to such abundant protein ensures survival.

The Wanderer likely wouldn't have encountered many bears anyway. Compared to the rest of Yukon Territory and Alaska, the Arctic supports relatively few bears. The poor quality of the habitat, molded by climate, topography, and vegetation, limits their numbers. Arctic grizzlies need a huge amount of land in order to gather enough to eat. Adult males have home ranges as large as 1,000 square miles, females from 140 to 340 square miles. Females with spring cubs have the smallest ranges, but as the cubs grow and demand more food, the size of their range increases. Within any home range, the actual area a bear uses for foraging, denning, and breeding is relatively small and often restricted to the river valleys. Given the low productivity of arctic plant biomes and the scarcity of fish that southern bears enjoy, grizzlies of the North Slope are much smaller than their coastal relatives, few weighing over six hundred pounds, and most females do not give birth until almost nine years of age. Arctic grizzlies have very low rates of reproductivity compared to more southerly populations.

Unlike wolves, who use speed to capture their quarry, bears rely on energy and stamina to run down their prey. In the Sadlerochit Mountains one spring, a hiker watched a grizzly bear climb an undulating ridge below a herd of several hundred caribou, many with days-old calves. The bear seemed to be in no particular hurry, stopping often to sniff the ground, dig roots, or graze the spring shoots. Then it ambled slowly over the ridge and out of sight. Perhaps it was unaware of the caribou above. Either way, the caribou never alerted.

A couple of hours later, however, the grizzly hurtled back over the ridge top, panicking the herd. They scattered, and the bear pursued a group racing uphill with one tiny calf struggling to keep up. Just when escape seemed impossible, the calf topped a slight ridge, then cut to the right to join another group plunging down a nearby swale. The grizzly crested the ridge and stopped; the calf was nowhere in sight. Nose to the ground, the bear began to cast about for the calf's scent. It found the scent trail but turned the wrong way, following its backtrail up and over the ridge.

The fragmented herd abandoned the slope and scattered onto flat tundra a mile or more away. An hour or so after the initial chase, the grizzly was again among them. Caribou scattered in all directions, some circling back toward the ridge. When a large segment of the herd began to coalesce, the bear charged, again fragmenting the group. The instinct to follow is powerful in caribou, even if it takes them closer to danger. Small bands and individuals doubled back to rejoin larger groups. The bear suddenly found itself the hub in the middle of a caribou wheel. Here was the bear's opportunity: a sharp turn would cut the intervening distance in half.

To the bear's right, a calf lagged behind its mother. The bear rushed toward it. When it stumbled in the tussocks, the grizzly pounced, crushing it to the ground. Twice the cow raced in, trying desperately to lure the bear away, but to no avail. In a matter of minutes, little was left of the calf, and the bear was curled up asleep nearby. All around the bear, scattered cows and calves wandered the tundra, the strident calling of separated pairs clearly audible.

In a period of four hours, the chase had covered at least five miles, some of it up and down a steep hillside and across tussock flats and marsh, draining a massive amount of the bear's energy in exchange for about ten pounds of protein. Other observers have seen bears pull down adult caribou after similar chases but for much greater rewards. Lame or diseased caribou seldom escape.

Wolves and bears compete for the same prey, and though in most cases they don't seem to be particularly wary of one another, conflict can arise over kills. The smell of blood, meat, or decay often brings the two together. A lone wolf has little chance to displace a grizzly from its quarry; a pack stands a better chance. In the reverse scenario, a grizzly may attempt to move a lone wolf off its kill but would fare poorly against a pack. Wolves appear to respect a grizzly's strength and power, but the wolf's superior agility and speed make for a natural advantage in any conflict. Even though he was powered by a reduced diet, the Wanderer was quick and agile enough to dodge any bear's lunge or attack.

The two predators become particularly mistrustful of one another in spring and summer, however, when rearing their young. Grizzlies with cubs are rightfully wary of wolves. A number of years ago, on a cool overcast July morning, a group of Denali National Park visitors witnessed a deadly confrontation between a pack of eleven wolves and a female grizzly with three yearling cubs. Near the East Fork River, a tour guide spotted the pack headed east, parallel to the road. In the creek bottom, well ahead of the wolves, the bear family ambled in the same direction. Because of a crosswind, the wolves may not have been aware of the bears traveling ahead of them.

A short while after the initial sighting, another tour guide spotted six members of the pack milling casually, wagging tails, and touching muzzles. She next sighted the bear family in a clearing a short distance upwind of the wolves. The yearling cubs appeared smaller than normal, weighing perhaps only forty or fifty pounds. The wolves soon caught scent of the bears and quickened their pace. When they spotted the bears, the wolves broke into a full charge. At first, the bears drew together but then bolted into the brush. Moments later they flushed into the open, all eleven wolves in close pursuit, some flanking the cubs, trying to separate them.

The mother attempted to defend her young, cutting between them and the attacking wolves. Several times she lunged at individual wolves, but the cubs would not stay together; as soon as she rescued one, she had to lurch off to save another. She quickly became disoriented and confused. She used up all her energy rushing from one cub to another. The wolves attacked her blind side, clearly intent on keeping her from her young.

Some distance from the road, the wolves drove the bears out of sight into a defile. Seconds later, one cub bolted from the depression, followed closely by the mother. The cub never hesitated but kept running. Its mother, however, stopped several times to look back for her two other cubs. She watched a large white wolf, likely the breeding female of the East Fork Pack, trot out of the defile with a large chunk of a cub in its mouth and settle down to eat it; other wolves soon straggled into the open and flopped down to rest. The female bear and her surviving cub escaped to the north. Witnesses said the entire incident took less than twenty minutes and "the whole process seemed damn easy for the wolves."

Wolves ferociously protect their pups and dens. Also in Denali National Park, a tour guide watched a grizzly approach the den of the Grant Creek Pack. The way the bear sniffed the air suggested that it was well aware of the den. But when it started to climb the slope toward the den, a huge black wolf, the pack's breeding male, burst from cover and hurtled into the bear's side, slashing with snapping jaws. The bear lunged for its attacker, but the wolf deftly dodged aside. Two more wolves quickly joined the attack. The black wolf was fearless in defense of the den and repeatedly closed on the bear, yanking out tufts of fur with each assault. The bear was soon in full rout, the wolves snapping at its flanks as it raced down the canyon.

Autumn challenges both bears and wolves preparing for the inevitable snow and cold. Bears gorge, then hibernate; wolves grow long thick coats to ward off the frost. Both face an added test: autumn is hunting season, a time when humans go afield in search of their own supply of winter meat. To date, the Wanderer had struggled to find food, competed with bears for caribou calves, and endured the torment of insatiable biting insects. He now faced an increased threat from people.

14

Open Season

All through August, the Wanderer remained within a relatively small territory, an area lying between the airstrips on the Ivishak River and Fin Creek, a tributary of the Shaviovik River. Fly-in hunters often landed here, and shallow-water boats plied the Ivishak. As the month progressed, and well into the next, more and more hunters arrived. Bull caribou had shed the velvet covering on their antlers and become prime targets. The Wanderer likely found and fed on their gut piles, which posed the grave risk of confrontation not only with bears but also with people—it is legal for hunters to shoot bears and wolves attracted to the offal of legally killed game.

These predators are often killed incidentally during caribou and moose hunts. Many sport hunters will not hesitate to shoot a wolf given the opportunity—a wolf pelt is considered a top trophy. They view wolves as competitors for wild game that need to be controlled or eliminated. Some hunters blame wolves for the lack of game or for an unsuccessful hunt. This is a perennial topic on public forums online; a typical comment reads, "Too many bears and wolfs. Would like to see a bounty on wolfs and bears, they kill off all our moose." Others think that the way wolves kill is cruel, often wasteful, and consequently undeserving of protection.

Alaska's wolf-hunting seasons are liberal and long. The season for wolves runs typically from August through April, with a limit of ten per hunter. Trapping season runs from November 1 to April 30, with no bag limit. Anyone can buy a trapping license, even if they have no intention of setting traps. Trapping license holders may also use firearms to shoot wolves, enabling incidental take whenever they are encountered.

Wolves also are targeted because of the common perception that they pose a danger to people. Although documented attacks on people are extremely rare, the fear of being injured or killed by a large carnivore, real or imagined, is a serious concern for some. In 2011, as the Wanderer roamed north from Yukon-Charley, that fear was running high.

ON MARCH 8, 2010, NEWS broke that a female jogger had been killed by wolves on a snow-covered road two miles from the remote village of Chignik Lake in southwest Alaska. According to initial reports, a pack of four wolves had attacked the woman, quickly overwhelming her. The news sparked headlines, intense news coverage, and volumes of online chatter, much of it wildly speculative. It was the first fatal wolf attack on a human in Alaska, and at that time only the second documented case of a nonrabid wild wolf killing a human in North America.

Investigators found no evidence that the wolves had attacked in self-defense or in defense of natural food sources. They also found no evidence of food attractants near the deceased or at the village. Prior to the attack, local residents infrequently saw wolves and usually only at a distance. The majority of attacks in North America involve wolves habituated to people and conditioned to associate humans with food. This attack did not fit that pattern.

A thorough investigation revealed additional details. The attack occurred in full daylight. Visibility was restricted by vegetation, road alignment, and possibly weather conditions. These factors, combined with the pattern of wolf tracks traveling toward the site of the attack, suggested that the wolves met the jogger head-on and did not stalk her from behind. Though a strong wind blowing in the wolves' general direction might have alerted them to her presence, the encounter appeared to have been a mutual surprise. The victim's initial reaction is unknown, but a flight response, or the appearance of one, could have elicited a predatory reaction by the wolves. The sight of a small running figure may have been the key trigger. Investigators considered it a rare event: an aggressive, predatory attack on a human by unhabituated wolves.

Because attacks on humans are infrequent and poorly understood, no one could predict if these wolves would engage in similar attacks. Authorities decided to cull those found in the immediate vicinity to address public safety concerns and collect biological forensic evidence. Eight wolves were killed in late March. Genetic analysis of samples taken from the victim and from the dead wolves positively identified one culprit, an adult female in excellent condition with no apparent health issues, and implicated others. This was the first case of a wolf attacking humans where DNA evidence was used for confirmation. Necropsies showed no abnormalities in any of the wolves, and no rabies or distemper. Based on the condition of the wolves and the number of prey species observed in the area, starvation or severe hunger did not appear to be a contributing factor. The final report on the tragedy was released in 2011, fueling anew the public debate over wolves.

The perceived threat posed by wolves, real or imagined, was nothing new to regulars on the Dalton Highway. The attack rekindled memories of several local incidents from five years earlier.

Early in the morning on July 7, 2006, a wolf attacked a woman as she walked near her campsite at Mile 115 on the Dalton Highway. The wolf chased her and bit her legs twice before she was able to escape to an outhouse at the Arctic Circle wayside. In the same area ten days later, a wolf approached a busload of tourists who were standing along the highway.

On the same day that the woman was attacked, a motorcyclist reported being chased by a wolf roughly thirty-five miles to the south, at Mile

79. Then, a week later in roughly the same location, a wolf pursued a fast-moving bicyclist. "He was catching up to me real quick," the cyclist reported. "I thought I could outrun him at first. . . . I know that's not what you're supposed to do, but I wasn't about to stop and get mauled." The wolf was gaining on him when a southbound freight truck swerved and struck it. The cyclist presumed that the trucker had deliberately hit the wolf, noting that the truck never stopped.

The wolf wasn't dead, but it was in bad shape. The cyclist and two other bikers who had trailed far behind dispatched the wolf with a knife. A subsequent necropsy found that its neck had been broken in the collision with the truck. The yearling female weighed just forty-six pounds and was probably starving to death. The wolf tested negative for rabies. A biologist believed it to be a different wolf than the one that had attacked the woman at the Arctic Circle wayside.

Why wolves had chased a pedestrian, motorcyclist, and bicyclist, as well as approached a group of tourists, was an open question. One possibility was that they had been fed by humans at some point and learned to associate vehicles or people with food.

In the wake of the Chignik Lake tragedy, wolves were increasingly targeted. According to official records, 1,166 wolves were killed in Alaska in 2010–11, 227 of the total in western and Arctic Alaska, nearly double the previous year. Fear, and perhaps retribution, motivated some of the killings.

THE OPEN TUNDRA OFFERED the Wanderer and other coursing wolves only faint concealment. For two days in early August, the Wanderer roamed near the Ivishak airstrip. Midmonth he loped right by the Fin Creek airstrip, an access point for caribou hunters. He was constantly on the move, which suggested he was hunting traveling caribou. By now, the Wanderer was in very poor condition and losing weight. He needed to make a kill soon in order to muster sufficient energy to keep hunting. His luck changed on August 19 when he lingered on a gravel bar on the Shaviovik River, just four miles west of the Fin Creek camp. He'd passed this same spot two days earlier, then abruptly retraced his steps. Perhaps he'd killed a caribou and then been scared off for some reason, or maybe he'd wounded dangerous prey and come back to claim it after it had weakened or died. In either scenario, data from his collar indicated possession of a large ungulate, his first major kill since June 27, fifty-four days earlier. Desperate to feed, the Wanderer tore into his catch.

Bears foraged these same gravel bars for squirrels and ripening soapberries. It would only be a matter of time before a bear, or other wolves, homed in on the scent. The Wanderer's good fortune held, however, and over the next five days he fed and rested near the kill.

Temperatures cooled throughout late August. The autumnal colors faded, and plants shed their leaves. Migrating waterfowl winged south over the mountains. Many shorebirds and songbirds were long gone. Daylight waned to little more than fifteen hours per day at month's end. On clear nights, the first stars and the faint glow of the aurora became visible overhead. Cold fronts delivered wind and clouds but little moisture. A light, transient snow fell on the far summits.

Well fed and rested, the Wanderer continued to hunt, but the last days of August were marked with fruitless chases for speedy prey. The calves had grown to half the size of their mothers, 125 pounds or so, and were equally difficult for the Wanderer to run down. On the flats, they had the advantage of speed; in the mountains, the balance shifted more toward the wolf. An abundance of prey seemed to hold him, and perhaps his partner, to the area, but he had little success catching anything.

Over the month, the Wanderer had rambled just 214 measurable miles, an average of 7.6 miles per day. Again, it appeared to biologists that he'd found prey, though he made few kills, and had claimed a territory and likely a running mate. But distance and fickle weather ruled out an overflight that could clarify the situation. Speculation centered on daily movements as the Wanderer responded to weather and the quickening pace of the caribou migration.

All across Alaska and northern Canada, young dispersers had roamed widely, found partners, claimed territory, and fended off other wolves, or been killed by them. Some died from starvation, accidents, disease, or injury inflicted by moose or bears. Others had been shot. Most had not gone far from their natal territories before settling in or dying. Few had traveled as far as the Wanderer had; the outcome of his long journey was still unknown.

15

Leaving the Tundra

The long miles and months of travel left visible marks on the Wanderer. Fresh cuts and abrasions on his muzzle and legs blended with older scars. A permanently dislocated toe caused a nail to elongate, more an occasional nuisance than a disability. On earlier forays across the high slopes, he had sliced his feet, and the tough pads were slow to heal. Some days he'd limp along with muscles wrenched in the unstable tussocks, although when he pursued prey, the lameness disappeared. He'd lost weight and his frame looked emaciated. At least his fur had lengthened and thickened, belatedly protecting him better from the last of the stinging insects and jagged plant stems that tore at him. Long hair filled out his mane and neck ruff, giving him the appearance of a much heavier animal. Now he sported a coat appropriate to the late autumn weather.

The Wanderer found the broad Arctic prairies taxing, one vast sea of sodden mat and tussock flats. Willow thickets, bristling with tough, dead branches sharp enough to penetrate flesh, lined many draws and watercourses. Rivers ran ice-cold, often deep and swift. Bogs and tundra tested and tortured the stamina and strength of even the peripatetic caribou. The wolf found the well-drained foothills and mountain slopes more stable and easier to traverse than the flat tundra.

Possessing legendary resilience, wolves are able to sustain cuts, wounds, injuries, and long periods of famine, yet keep on running. It is a perilous life taking down large prey with your mouth, competing for and defending territory against neighboring packs, and shielding kills from bears. The ability to sustain physical injuries and go hungry for long periods is crucial to survival. No wolf goes through life without injury, and old wolves—those over eight—are lean, battle-scared veterans of the rugged northern wilderness.

To sustain the strength and energy to eke out a livelihood in the far north, wolves must eat, and to eat, they must always be on the move. They survive by marking their territory, circling again and again over the same terrain, watching, sensing, and always seeking. Much of a wolf's prey is alert, wary, elusive, and often scarce, as they, too, move long distances in search of forage that is only seasonally abundant. A wolf unable to travel faces certain death.

Some caribou still roamed the tundra uplands. The weather had turned unusually mild and relatively warm, slowing the herd's southward flow. Mercifully, a series of frosts in early September had ended mosquito season, and the roving animals grazed in peace, piling on fat for the rigors of rut and the coming winter. Their constant search for food kept the Wanderer on the move. The tundra that he roamed between the Ivishak and Shaviovik Rivers was smack in the traditional path of the Central Arctic Herd's move south from the coast. Over much of the terrain, the long-legged caribou easily outran, or outlasted, the pursuing wolf.

The herd often moves south in a steady pulse of small bands, rather than in one mass movement, from September through early November, typically before snow accumulates and hinders travel. Older, experienced cows lead the migration, and younger animals learn the traditional routes by example. Unseasonable storms often accelerate the southward flow, though severe weather may impede or delay them. But not this year. As the month progressed, daily temperatures rarely topped 40°F and dipped into the high twenties at night. Once they are underway, it takes about two weeks or less for the Central Arctic Herd to reach their winter range, their speed and movement influenced by the search for optimal forage and weather.

With climate change threatening to fragment habitats and create obstacles to future migrations, caribou's dependence on current routes may hinder their ability to adapt. The timing of the Central Arctic Herd's migration has varied in response to altered weather patterns in the years since the Wanderer hunted the northern tundra. In 2020, the herd largely wintered north of the Brooks Range.

AS AUTUMN SLIPPED AWAY, overcast leaden skies brought a damp chill to the tundra. On rare clear days, the sun lost its edge, the morning mists burning away only in late afternoon. Blizzards of leaves fell under the faintest breeze, and whole hillsides turned stark and bare in minutes. Summer forage faded and lost value as it shriveled, died, and moldered. Many nights, swirling fog glazed the sere grasses and sedges with hoarfrost. Frozen vegetation crackled and shattered when the Wanderer trod over it. The skim ice on shadowed pond edges never melted but was too thin to support the wolf when he crept down to drink. Silence reigned on those windless mornings; birds and their songs had gone south on the wind. Only an occasional flight of migrating tundra swans or the alarm bark of a red fox broke the deep hush. Infrequently, the distant howling of wolves froze the Wanderer in his tracks.

Except for a twenty-mile jaunt on September 9, the Wanderer moved only short distances the first two weeks of the month, averaging around ten miles per day. His roving, though limited, gave no indication of another successful hunt. In midmonth, he began to expand his peregrinations, roaming from an extensive aufeis flat on the Echooka River to a 3,500-foot slope in the Philip Smith Mountains twelve air miles to the south. From there, he turned around and went right back north fourteen miles to the mouth of Fin Creek. Over the next ten days, he crisscrossed familiar tundra but frequently returned to the Echooka River drainage, the south end of his usual range. The weather cooled as the month wore on, but with only minimal precipitation. Daylight waned rapidly as temperatures dipped; on the autumnal equinox, the low was 31°F, with low clouds scudding across the tundra and mountains.

For almost two months, the Wanderer had roamed an area of 1,039 square miles—a fairly typical territory for a wolf pack—and other wolves had not displaced him. Biologist John Burch thought the wolf's fidelity to a fixed territory to be a strong indicator that he had partnered up, but he harbored doubts. The wolf's minimal hunting success hinted that he was alone. Taking down adult mammals is no easy task for a single wolf. Perhaps the concentration of caribou appealed to him even though he'd struggled over the last two months to acquire food. Burch knew that wolves don't necessarily kill as many adult prey animals in summer as they do in winter; in summer they subsist on the seasonal bounty of young mammals and birds. Perhaps, along with the migrating caribou, abundant ptarmigan, rodents, and carrion rooted the wolf to the area. There is no way to know for sure.

Other wolves must have navigated the same terrain. The presence of caribou in numbers, even if just passing through, would have attracted them. Earlier, in the Arctic National Wildlife Refuge, the Wanderer had traversed the territories of several resident packs, as well as others to the refuge's west. The Arctic packs are quite small, fewer than five or so, their numbers determined by prey density. Now freed of the demands of spring pup rearing, they would be ranging widely. Contact seemed likely if not inevitable. Two traditional dens were about a long day's trot away. Even for a pair of wolves, interaction with a hunting pack would be perilous. To date, he had been smart, stealthy, and lucky to avoid violent contact; or with a partner or partners, he had been able to defend the territory. Again, evidence was scant.

As September wore on, the caribou migration picked up speed. After the summer feeding season, most were in prime condition, fast and strong.

The caribou rut would soon begin, perhaps even with the fall migration still underway. Bands now passed rapidly through the Wanderer's area, but they did not linger.

Muskox were also on the move. Bachelor bulls had grazed the tundra terraces along the Ivishak drainage through most of the summer, but in the middle of August, they had begun to seek out groups of females. The first order of business for a dominant bull entering a herd is to drive out other males; those head-battering battles sometimes decide the issue. Muskox breeding season picks up steam through September and wanes in early October. Breeding bulls are irascible and extremely aggressive during the rut and chase off any other animal that approaches, even foxes and birds. Experienced wolves avoid them.

Throughout the third week of September, with the temperatures dipping lower and the terrain emptying of prey, the Wanderer remained fairly close to the Echooka drainage. He meandered an average of just 3.7 miles per day, less than 23 total miles. The short movements suggested that he may have been scavenging carrion, making only short forays away to rest or avoid competitors. He also may have been searching for something else. Was he just combing for offal, or had he lost his partner?

On September 24, the temperature dropped at night into the single digits, the autumn aging into something raw and punishing, and the first real hint of winter broke over the hills, with the tundra cold and heavy, smelling of snow. Ravens, ever ubiquitous, wheeled on the unyielding wind. The Wanderer abandoned his territory for the final time that day. The morning hours found him twenty-seven miles south as the raven flies, clambering over ice-slick talus on a 3,900-foot slope on the north side of the upper Ivishak River. The overnight trek was his longest one-day movement since July 16.

What precipitated the Wanderer's move is unknown. Did the scarcity of prey trigger his departure? Had he been chased off by an encounter with another pack? If he'd paired up, had his partner been killed by other wolves? Or by people? Later that winter, someone posted photos online of wolves killed by hunters near the Ivishak. One was of "two wolves killed out of a pack of three," but the connection to the Wanderer is tenuous, likely dubious. Months earlier, after his running mate, Wolf 227, had died in Yukon-Charley, the Wanderer vacated the area, moving miles to the west. If in fact he'd lost a partner, it meant that he'd lost two potential mates in less than eight months. His response both times was movement, swift and far.

Whatever had pushed him south, researchers knew within days that the Wanderer was alone and unlikely to return to the territory he'd called home for nearly two months.

16

South Through the Boreal Mountains

On the second day of his journey south, the Wanderer traveled twenty-four air miles to the drainage of the Saviukviayak River, taking him straight through the Philip Smith Mountains, a striking massif rising from the tundra uplands. On the 26th, the Wanderer trotted up a rocky creek bed draining from five-thousand-foot mountains, on the south side of the Ribdon River and ten miles east of Elusive Lake.

His next move was somewhat puzzling. In autumn, the Ribdon River is often a major, perhaps critical, route for migrating caribou. Mountain passes at the head lead southeast into the Junjik River and Chandalar drainages. Earlier in the summer, the Wanderer had traversed these same hillsides near the passes. Now, although much of the migrating caribou had preceded him up the Ribdon and through the mountains to the southeast, the Wanderer veered south, perhaps on the scent trail left by a few following a different route. Whatever the reason, he'd deviated from the path taken by the bulk of his prey. Judging by his recent movements, the Wanderer appeared unimpaired by injury or hunger; his days were long, his route strenuous.

Later that day, the Wanderer loped past one of the most significant archaeological sites in Alaska, a high bench where some of North America's first inhabitants, the Paleoindians, once lived. Fifty years ago, archaeologists located the remnants of an ancient campsite on a knoll eight hundred feet above the upper Sagavanirktok River and uncovered several stone projectile points, the oldest dating back 10,500 years. They also identified artifacts from two other periods, one back 8,500 years and another of historic vintage. This site, known as the Putu site, and the more famous Mesa site 150 miles to the west offer important clues to and inform our understanding of when the first people arrived in the Western Hemisphere. Prior to the sites' discovery, archaeologists generally believed that the peopling of North America was a single migration out of Asia. But the distinctiveness of the stone points found in these Arctic sites indicated that there may have been several migrations. (Mesa artifacts range in date from 9,700 to 11,700 years old and closely resemble Paleoindian tools found far to the south.) Scientists now believe migration into Beringia more likely involved many back-and-forth movements rather than a single eastward thrust. Early Alaska may have been occupied by multiple cultures who spoke different languages, had distinct ways of making tools, and were based primarily on hunting ice age animals, including now-extinct bison, mammoth, and horses. The Late Pleistocene wolf, the forerunner of today's gray wolf, was a fierce competitor for meat. Since the very onset of human occupation of North America, wolves have shared the landscape.

By September 27, the Wanderer moved another thirty-five air miles to the south side of the Continental Divide, well beyond the headwaters of the Sagavanirktok River. That subfreezing morning found him traversing a 4,391-foot hillside, sixteen miles east of the Chandalar Shelf airstrip on the Dalton Highway. This 3,000-foot plateau at the headwaters of a fork of the Chandalar River was sometimes traversed by caribou pushing southeast to winter range and driven by the stirrings of the rut, but few had passed this way.

In the ragged, gray, snow-lashed mountains, the Wanderer found little to eat. Ground squirrels had gone underground, ptarmigan were scattered and few, and small numbers of Dall sheep scaled their escape terrain. A plump, ten-pound Alaska marmot would have made a satisfying meal, but they, too, were beneath the rocks, snug in their grass-lined burrows. This unique subspecies, also called the Brooks Range marmot, hibernates for much of the year, usually beginning at the first hint of winter. The Wanderer crossed silent talus slopes, the predator alarm calls of the marmot colonies stilled by sleep.

What *was* the wolf eating? The dearth of location clusters, as recorded by his satellite collar, indicated a continuing struggle to find food. Daily he was traveling distances not recorded since midsummer. The day-by-day totals seemed to indicate strength and good health, but how much longer could he continue without finding substantial nourishment?

After leaving the Chandalar Shelf, the Wanderer trotted fifteen more miles south through the snowy mountains above the North Fork Chandalar River. This was prime Dall sheep country and mountain terrain similar to the wolf's natal range far to the southeast. A couple of years later, in 2013, a delayed spring would kill off many of the sheep in this region, but now they were still fairly plentiful. He then did an about-face and retraced his steps north four miles, as the raven flies, to a rocky tributary of Your Creek. Perhaps a long chase or strong scent trail enticed him there, but he did not tarry. He soon turned right around and headed south again, traversing ridges that climbed to 6,500 feet and then descending to cross the frigid North Fork Chandalar River, not far from Reds Lake. October 1 turned cold, the low just 13°F, with a light snow adding to the inch or so already blanketing the slopes.

That night, with snow beginning to accumulate, the wolf loped twenty-seven more miles south through high mountains to the confluence of Woodland Echo Creek and the North Fork Chandalar River, just downstream of the Chandalar Lake outlet. By morning the next day, three inches of new snow had fallen and the temperature was zero, with a rim of ice circling the lake.

The Wanderer had moved into one of the most spectacular mountain settings on the south slope of the Brooks Range. Chandalar Lake, sixty-five air miles east of the village of Wiseman on the Dalton Highway, is nestled in a high valley fringed with scattered spindly spruce pocking the tundra where caribou sometimes winter, but they were then scarce. Autumn colors intensify here in early September, and snow often buries the fading crimson and gold leaves.

Hunting and trapping have long been part of the way of life at Chandalar. The late Wayne "Red" Adney operated a hunting lodge here. He first came to Wiseman in 1934 to mine but, finding the best ground already claimed, moved on to Chandalar Lake in January 1935. Adney worked alongside other miners on some relatively poor gold claims on a feeder stream, Indian Creek. As was the custom in those days, he turned to trapping to supplement his income with fur sales and the bounty on wolves. He found the area to be relatively poor fur country, but he trapped far up the North Fork from his cabin on Chandalar Lake. During his excursions, he identified excellent sheep habitat and many large rams, later exploiting the knowledge as a sport hunting guide.

During World War II, Adney joined the famed Alaskan Scouts, known as "Castner's Cutthroats," a combat intelligence platoon of the Alaska Command, which consisted of various pioneer outdoorsmen. After the war, he obtained his guide's license and eventually became a master guide. Adney trapped and shot wolves but would not kill anything near his cabins on Chandalar Lake or allow anyone else to do so. For a couple of years, a black wolf came by to feed on scraps he had thrown out. One day, a Fairbanks pilot landed on the airstrip and shot the wolf; Adney delivered a blistering tirade and banned him from landing on the strip. Adney eventually sold his lodge and guiding business. A modern fly-in lodge carries on a version of the traditional land use.

In March 2013, two wolves—"acting wild, unafraid, and crazy," according to a witness—approached a cabin on the west side of the lake. Both wolves had rabies and were later shot by a trapper, one of them caught in a trap. Before they were killed, they had ripped apart a family pet, a Pomeranian.

Until then, rabies had not previously been diagnosed south of the Brooks Range, but veterinarians say that rabies was likely present in the canid population well before this incident, which means that the Wanderer faced this risk as he passed through the area. The rabies diagnosis triggered a scare among pet owners and prompted rabies vaccination clinics in Fairbanks and other Interior communities.

THE WANDERER LEFT THE LAKE and moved off downstream, a sun dog in the hazy sky hinting at the long, dark winter closing in. All too soon, persistent icy winds would deliver more snow and make food for grazers ever harder to find in the Chandalar district. He paused several times on his journey to strip blueberries desiccated by the wind and cold, but securing prey was critical for his survival as the north drifted deeper toward the fierce cold.

On the south side of the Brooks Range, the wolf was again below the tree line, where the chatter of red squirrels betrayed his passage. Once, the amber eyes of a great gray owl tracked his transit through the timber. Beneath other shadowed spruce, the Wanderer trotted by tiny boreal owls hunting red-backed voles, which were also favored by the much larger great gray. Ravens, those pervasive scavengers, spotted him and trailed along, hoping to pilfer scraps.

The fresh snow displayed a calligraphy of large and small tracks for the Wanderer—and other predators—to decipher and perhaps investigate. Any scent, sound, or sight of prey, no matter how faded or faint, could now alter the wolf's journey, perhaps even his life.

17

Crossing the Circle

In the lower valley of the South Fork Koyukuk River, the terrain was snow-free, wet, and soggy from recent melt. Gone was the brilliant autumnal palette, replaced by a chiaroscuro dreariness. A relentless northeast wind drove blizzards of withered leaves, shearing clean the alders and willows. Dark clouds tore on the flanking, crenelated summits, threatening more snow and cold. On the south side of the range, vegetation was taller and denser. Tangles of sere plants, interspersed with black spruce and skeletal poplar, choked the flats lining the waterways, forcing the Wanderer to either stay on the hillsides or negotiate twisting game trails through the thickets.

On October 2, the Wanderer traced the North Fork Chandalar River downstream from Chandalar Lake, then veered west to wade through icy Crooked Creek. He continued southwest, passing through Boatman Pass to a ridge just east of the South Fork Koyukuk, a one-day journey of almost twenty-seven miles. Until now, the Wanderer had cut southward straight through the mountains, but this time, he traversed a drainage and then a ridgeline, a more typical travel pattern for a wolf. He'd averaged twenty-one miles per day since leaving the North Slope nine days earlier and still seemed strong, unaffected by hunger.

If the wolf was hunting caribou, he'd come to the wrong place. Huge herds had once migrated into the valley of the Koyukuk, but no longer. A lifelong resident of Wiseman village remembers those big herds and marks 1973 as the last year of abundance. They apparently shifted ranges east and west, and for more than three decades, by his reckoning, the caribou had failed to show up at all. Locals blamed the construction of the pipeline haul road in 1974 for the change.

Whatever the reason—construction of the pipeline and haul road, vegetation changes due to the warming climate, or a natural shift in the migration pattern—vast herds of caribou seldom congregate on the lower South Fork or Middle Fork Koyukuk. In recent years, small groups have passed through, but not in the numbers once seen. The valley, however, is moose country, home to formidable beasts with antlers stretching over five feet. A wolf's universe is a galaxy of scent, an olfactory acuity beyond human comprehension. It uses scent to find its way; locate other wolves, territories, and food; and respond to danger. In these willows, in this valley, a pervasive but familiar odor, one the Wanderer had not detected or savored in weeks, energized and perhaps even tormented him: *moose*.

The scent of moose, flowing from all directions, was strong in the brush. Signs were everywhere: pruned willows and poplar, fresh tracks etched in the river sand over older ones, tufts of hair wobbling on the breeze, and piles of grape-sized pellets. Broken saplings lent silent testimony to the recent rut and the ravages of a bull polishing his antlers. Muddy wallows still gave off the pungent, powerful aroma of bulls where they'd stomped in their scent to energize the cows. Moose were here, more than a few. If only the Wanderer could kill one, the carcass would feed him for days, maybe weeks. But alone, he was no match for a bull rising silently, hackles raised, out of a darkened wood. Perhaps, he would find one wounded during the rut and injured enough to bring down, or maybe the ubiquitous ravens would lead him to a carcass left from a violent battle. Other wolves hunted here, as well as a few bears still active before hibernation. Contesting a kill would be risky for the Wanderer.

Moose eluded the hunting wolf as he scoured the thickets on his journey south. Likely he flushed a few from hiding and tested them, but none were weak enough to be overcome. To maintain his strength, the Wanderer needed food, but even small game was scarce. The Koyukuk periodically supports numerous snowshoe hares, feeding an array of predators. A few could tide the Wanderer over until he secured something larger. The willow brush along the forks of the Koyukuk bore old scars from ravenous hares, with dead and girdled stems evidence of past overbrowsing. Just now, however, hares were almost nonexistent. From 2002 to 2015, the hare population on the Koyukuk remained rock-bottom, at the extreme low end of their cycle.

The miles the Wanderer had traversed, without eating much, had cost him weight. Biologists, when examining dead wolves, often describe their condition as "lean but good"—a rather meaningless description. There simply are no *fat* wolves. All wolves are lean, and it would not be an exaggeration to say that they are always on the edge of starvation. A sudden scarcity of game, a muscle injury, a kick from a moose, or an encounter with a porcupine, and a lingering death is inevitable.

If he was desperate enough, the Wanderer would attack almost anything, even a porcupine. The North American porcupine carries about thirty thousand quills, each one studded near the tip with between seven hundred and eight hundred barbs. The tiny fishhook-like barbs help the quills move deeper into the tissue, eventually penetrating into body cavities and internal organs. Because the quills carry bacteria, they also serve as a source of infection and abscesses, which may lead to lethal, systemic complications. Porcupines don't throw or shoot their quills but rather pound them into an attacker with a slap of their tail. A biting animal like a wolf that gets a face and mouth full of spines is bound to suffer a prolonged, excruciating death, as was the case for a member of the Edwards Creek Pack.

Like the Wanderer, the early human residents of the Koyukuk drainage had also known famine. An Iñupiat resident of Wiseman, Kalhabuk (Florence Jonas), who was in her mideighties when she died in 1979, followed the traditional nomadic ways of Native caribou hunters for the first two decades of her life. Famine was commonplace in the subsistence culture, and Kalhabuk nearly starved in four different winters when her people couldn't find caribou. During one winter famine, she reportedly cut the hair off her animal-skin clothing and boiled and ate it in order to survive. Human or wolf, the Arctic plays no favorites.

Judging by the Wanderer's daily movements, he was not finding or killing anything substantial. Perhaps he caught a spruce grouse or two or a few meadow voles, but that would only amplify his hunger, not alleviate it. If he chose now to turn due west and cross the Dalton Highway, he would need to travel nearly 150 miles in order to reach the wintering grounds of the giant Western Arctic Caribou Herd, then about 325,000 strong. Those intervening miles led not to the caribou themselves but to their *traditional* wintering grounds; as elsewhere, their movements had been unpredictable in recent years. Instead, he veered south, again avoiding the highway and human activity.

On October 3, the Wanderer was a short day's trot away from Coldfoot truck stop on the Dalton Highway, a few miles downstream from the village of Wiseman. Situated along the Middle Fork Koyukuk River, Wiseman is about sixty miles north of the Arctic Circle, just three miles off the highway, and near the boundary of Gates of the Arctic National Park and Preserve. The village sprang up around 1909, a result of the Nolan Creek gold discovery. The population has fluctuated over the years, from its heyday in the 1920s as a mining and trading outpost to its current population of about a dozen residents. Many of the original gold rush–era cabins are still in use today.

The Koyukuk mining district was one of Alaska's most isolated areas, and one of the most expensive to develop. Residents lived off the land as much as possible, hunting, trapping, and berry picking. Natives and newcomers lived in a rather harmonious community largely free of the typical turmoil of frontier mining camps. One notable visitor, forester Robert Marshall, detailed the unique lifeways of the people of Wiseman in his 1933 best-selling book *Arctic Village*.

Marshall was born January 2, 1901, in New York City and spent summers at his family's home in the Adirondack Mountains, where he eventually climbed all forty-six Adirondack peaks above four thousand feet. In 1924, Marshall graduated magna cum laude from Syracuse with a bachelor's degree in forestry and later earned a doctorate in forestry at Johns Hopkins. In all, Marshall made three privately financed trips to the central Brooks Range, penning numerous articles about his travels.

Marshall served as head of recreation management in the Forest Service from 1937 until his death in 1939, shaping the department's policy on wilderness designation and management. He wrote ardently on all aspects of conservation and preservation and was among the first to suggest that large tracts of Alaska be preserved. His writings focused on the aesthetic value of wilderness to humankind and pushed for public ownership. In 1935, Marshall and other pioneer wilderness activists created the Wilderness Society. Twenty-five years after his death from heart failure, the Wilderness Society celebrated the passage of the Wilderness Act. Montana's Bob Marshall Wilderness Complex honors his legacy of wilderness preservation.

THE WANDERER WAS IN UNKNOWN country and had to find food—and soon—to survive the looming winter. Day by day, winter closed on the land. The hills and valleys lay stark and bare. On clear nights, countless stars winked amid wavering auroral bands that shifted from lime to crimson, bright enough at times to light the ground. Overhead, the Big Dipper and Cassiopeia circled Polaris, the North Star, brilliant in the cosmic cold.

Only luck and constant movement would keep the Wanderer alive. He continued his run southward, the next day climbing into the foothills lining the upper Jim River, nine miles due east of Grayling Lake on the

Dalton Highway. His travel pattern using ridges and watercourses was again more typical of his kind. Overnight he'd traced the Mosquito Fork of the South Fork Koyukuk River downstream to near Eagle Cliff, where he then turned up a small tributary that drained the foothills above the Jim River. He continued through a low pass, where perhaps he scented small clusters of Dall sheep. Sheep range is limited here, the animals never numerous. Fleet, swift, and sure-footed across the rocky slopes, they eluded him. His tracking collar gave no evidence that he caught one.

With each passing day, the wolf's competition for food lessened. Already bears clawed aside soil, rocks, and the roots of trees to burrow in for their long winter sleep. The Wanderer and other wolves would be the only apex predators about for the next few grueling months, tested by hunger, darkness, the searing wind, and the stabbing cold. A pack, with its ability to bring down moose, stands a much greater chance of surviving winter than a solitary wolf.

By the following morning, the Wanderer had loped another twenty-four miles south, wading through frigid Prospect Creek, then the twin forks of Bonanza Creek, to reach the divide above Fish Creek. He kept moving and had run thirteen more miles by the morning of October 6, crossing the Arctic Circle for the second time in his life. At dawn he trotted up the long inclines to the plateaus of the Hodzana Hills, at the head of the Kanuti River, on the western boundary of the Yukon Flats National Wildlife Refuge. The Hodzana Hills—drained by the Dall and Hodzana Rivers on the east and the Kanuti River and smaller drainages on the west—rise to about four thousand feet in elevation, their open tundra summits marked with distinct granite tors.

The wolf again coursed open, treeless tundra as he gained altitude and left the willow and forest fringe behind. Frost heaves, tussocks, and solifluction terraces and lobes gave witness to the extreme winter temperatures that shaped the Hodzana Hills. Alaska's all-time cold temperature of -80°F was set on January 23, 1971, at Prospect Creek Camp, just a few miles northwest of the wolf's current location.

Below and to the west, the Kanuti River meandered across a four-mile-wide tundra flat dotted with wetlands and small lakes. Spindly spruce and poplar lined segments of the river, but bog, cotton grass, and sedges dominated the otherwise treeless expanse. On the flats, Olsons Lake was largely a broad spot in the river and marsh, a remnant of a once-much-larger water body.

Of all the directions the Wanderer could have gone, he'd somehow ended up in these hills, in the vicinity of a small, nonmigratory caribou herd of around a thousand animals scattered across windswept rocky uplands. But did he háve the speed and vitality to catch and kill one? Surely, his long fast had sapped his strength.

The origin of the Hodzana Hills Herd, as well as three other small herds just north of the Yukon River, is unknown. Some residents speculate they derived from a reindeer herding operation in the Kokrines Hills that ended around 1935. Traditional knowledge suggests that these animals are simply relict populations of once vast herds that migrated across western Alaska. In the 1920s, Olaus Murie called the Hodzana Hills "the center of abundance for caribou" north of the Yukon.

Infrequently, small groups feed away from the hills and onto the Kanuti River flats. Sometimes they are seen along the Dalton Highway near Finger Mountain, or south of Caribou Mountain on the west side of the highway. Since the herd does not migrate, these forays are infrequent and forage related. Hunters access these caribou primarily by aircraft, with occasional approaches from the road; they harvest just two or three animals annually.

The rut was on, and groups of bulls and cows milled about in scattered locations. The bands are a whirl of activity as dominant males approach and pester the estrous, or near-estrous, females. The breeding bulls attack and repulse the smaller bulls that orbit the bands as they attempt to gain access to the females. Unlike many other members of the deer family, bull caribou do not control a harem of cows but instead guard an area around themselves, preventing others from breeding with the females within that zone. Bulls use their hooves and outsized antlers for fighting, and the largest dominant males do most of the breeding. Most fights between bulls are brief, the winner determined after lightning-fast antler clashes and powerful thrusting back and forth. Other battles are prolonged and vicious. In rare instances, bulls lock their antlers together and are unable to break apart, a death sentence for both animals.

Entering the rut, bull caribou are in the fattest and best shape of the year after the summer feeding and growing season. Many of the mature bulls pack on more than three inches of fat on their back and rump, energy for the rut. Ironically, despite being in prime condition, these bulls are slower than in other seasons. The extra weight slows them and causes them to overheat, negating some of their speed advantage over wolves. The breeding bulls expend vast amounts of energy this time of year; afterward, all are in a weakened condition. Nonbreeding bulls usually come through the rut in better shape. Some bulls suffer serious, debilitating injuries; a few are even killed. Locating just such a bull is what the Wanderer desperately needed now.

On the 7th, the wolf moved back north a few miles and remained there the next day. It is doubtful that he made his own kill, but instead he likely found the remains of a recently killed caribou. Something rooted him to that open, wind-blasted slope for a short time. Two days later, he meandered the highlands above the Kanuti River headwaters, just ten miles east of Finger Mountain. The name Kanuti comes from the local Athabascan *Kk'toonootne*, which translates to "well-traveled river by both man and animals." An early day explorer translated the word as "Old Man's River," which would account for the alternate name "Old Man River" used by pioneer prospectors. These barren uplands were well traveled by the Wanderer until the 11th, when the weather turned colder, down to 12°F, with snow, the chill typical of the long, dark days of winter. Judging by the lack of location clusters recorded by his tracking collar, the wolf had failed to make another kill or find more carrion.

Under falling snow, the wolf abandoned the Hodzana Hills to run twenty-one air miles due south to the low, open ridges of the Fort Hamlin Hills, about two miles east of the Dalton Highway and sixteen miles north of the Yukon River. (The hills take their name from a long-abandoned Alaska Commercial Company trading post, Fort Hamlin, built in 1899, on the Yukon River's south bank.) It appeared the Wanderer was beelining for the Yukon River, perhaps to return to his old territory in the eastern Tanana Hills. Researchers have documented other dispersers that have returned home after months away. Canids, as most people know from lost-dog stories, possess an astounding sense of direction. Might he be headed home? Wolves seem always tempted by far horizons but also drawn back to familiar haunts.

Whether he moved down to the banks of the Yukon, or even saw it for the first time in months, is unknown, but he was close enough to scent its rich earthy smell. There were no caribou here, nor moose on the treeless ridges. No sign of prey held him or pulled him south. He turned back north and by the morning of the 12th had retraced his steps ten miles, as the raven flies, to a tundra creek bottom four miles east of the Dalton Highway.

Near the Arctic Circle, the days were barely nine hours long, but a wolf doesn't need daylight to travel. That night under a full moon, the Hunter's Moon, the Wanderer loped back to the Kanuti uplands to the same ridge where'd lingered for two days earlier in the week, lured by the memory or scent of food. Since wolves often return to where they have fed before, he may have gnawed old bones or pawed through beds of hair searching for scraps, anything edible. By now, his hunger was intense, his situation growing dire.

Over the next three days, the Wanderer roved only short distances around the uplands, never going more than a couple of miles a day. His short movements were a puzzle. Was something amiss? Or was he alerting to prey? Picking over old kills? Hunting ptarmigan? One thing was certain: *he needed food*.

On the ridges above the Kanuti, a sudden lethargy overtook the Wanderer. His vitality and strength ebbed away—he grew listless and weak. An

unfamiliar languor made every motion a struggle. If he saw other predators, he hardly responded, his flight response sapped. Every movement
was slow and deliberate; caribou could have wandered close by, but he had
no chance of catching one.

Sometime on October 16, the wolf descended from the uplands, going
straight downhill to the north bank of the Kanuti River, just upstream of
the Dalton Highway bridge. Spindly spruce dotted the winding oxbows of
the river running with ice, and the surrounding tundra was blanketed with
two inches of new snow.

Perhaps the Wanderer followed a few caribou moving downhill to forage. It was not the odor of spawned-out fish that lured him; no salmon
reproduced here. Only twice have chum salmon spawned on the Kanuti
River, both locations well downstream and west of the highway bridge.
More than likely, moving downhill took the least energy.

The 17th dawned in a blizzard, the temperature 20°F. The wolf was just
one mile northeast of the Dalton Highway, as close as he is known to have
gotten to that roadway. If he regained his strength, would he cross it? Enter
the Kanuti River National Wildlife Refuge? Roam west into the Ambler
River drainage? If not, then where?

Late that night, under a wind-torn sky, the Wanderer wobbled up the
soggy marsh that edged the river, the waning Hunter's Moon lighting the
way. A few hundred feet from where he had been the night before, he collapsed, exhausted, under the spare, sheltering limbs of a spruce tree. On
his side, nose into the wind, he blinked and the world came into focus. He
could see spruce needles dark and sharp against the faint sky. A hard gust
shook the limbs; he heard the rustle and felt pelting ice. One last breath,
and he was still.

WHEN BIOLOGIST JOHN BURCH reviewed the tracking data, he saw that on
October 18, Wolf 258's collar began transmitting in what biologists call

"mortality mode," south of the Brooks Range, not far below the Arctic Circle.

Some days later, on a subzero morning, with a slicing northeast wind scaling the snow from the tundra, field assistant Seth McMillan left the Dalton Highway on skis. The oxbows and sloughs of the Kanuti River were frozen over and the wind unrelenting, the skiing marginal over tundra covered with a few inches of patchy snow.

On the riverbank, McMillan checked his receiver for the wolf's signal. He had to be careful in the blistering wind; exposed skin would freeze in seconds. He found the Wanderer under a gnarled, stunted spruce. "The wolf was completely covered with two-inches of snow, frozen on his side, head back and nose into the wind, tail still curled over him. The first thing I noticed was his long claws, maybe two inches long, curled down and over his pads, a sign of extreme nutrient deficiency. John Burch had told me that he was a fairly large male, but when I picked him up, he was so light, I knew he'd starved."

Over all those long miles, the Wanderer had negotiated the home ranges of dozens of wolves, made passing contact with grizzlies, survived human hunters and disease, and provoked moose and muskox, but in the end, a lack of food defeated his phenomenal stamina and strength. We'll never know the Wanderer's intentions when he turned away from the Yukon River and headed back north to the Hodzana Hills. For weeks his life had been defined and nourished by caribou. Perhaps if he'd managed to kill one and recover his strength before going south, he'd have crossed the Yukon and made it back home.

Epilogue

When Wolf 258 braved the pounding ice of the Yukon River on April 30, 2011, leaving his natal territory for good, he became a disperser, explorer, wayfarer, traveler, and wanderer, thus inspiring his nickname. Wildlife biologists prefer simple numerical identifiers, such as Wolf 227 or Wolf 258. Every study animal, from birds to bears, gets one. Even supreme ocean hunters like orcas get a prosaic number—AJ17, for example (member 17 of the AJ pod). No Willy or Moby Dick, just digits. The name "the Wanderer," used for Wolf 258 throughout this book (despite some pushback from biologists), is a rather neutral but accurate name that describes this wolf's remarkable journey.

In less than six months, Wolf 258 had covered 2,085 *measured* miles but as many as 1.42 times more, for an estimated total of 2,960. GPS tracking collars only measure point-to-point distances, their actual meanders between unknown. Across all those miles, the wolf never crossed a road nor private land. He never once had to seek "permission" to continue while traversing millions of acres of public lands. Nowhere else in the United States is such a journey even remotely possible. In the Lower 48, the farthest a creature can get from a road is twenty-one miles, in Yellowstone National Park.

The Wanderer's long journey coursed through some of the richest wildlife habitat in Alaska, millions of acres of wilderness, for hundreds of thousands of caribou, tens of thousands of moose, and thousands of sheep—and yet he starved. Well-known wolf researcher L. David Mech once said that a wolf usually dies either of starvation or by being killed by other wolves. Between the time when he was collared and when he was found dead, the Wanderer had lost nearly a third of his body weight.

A necropsy of the Wanderer, conducted on November 29, 2011, by the ADF&G, revealed no evidence of rabies or distemper. Elongated claws and a dislocated toe were the only structural abnormalities. His gut was loaded with tapeworms, not unexpected, and his stomach was full of a brown fluid, his stool black and tarry. Severe stomach ulcers showed the potential for a protein-losing enteropathy and bleeding into the gut. We do not know which came first, ulceration or starvation. At the time of capture, his testes measured 4.7 centimeters by 2.56 centimeters, small for a wolf his age. By the time he died, they had shrunk almost to nothing, possibly due to starvation as the body mobilized protein to survive. He weighed just sixty-nine pounds.

The Wanderer is just one of hundreds of wolves collared by researchers over the last few decades. In many ways, his story is unique but also typical of dispersing wolves. The sheer distances he covered are phenomenal, but likely other wolves have gone as far, or farther, and explored as much only to end up dead or successfully building a new pack. Data gathered using new technology is shedding light on behaviors that in the past we could only guess at.

The Yukon-Charley Rivers National Preserve's wolf study is the third-longest-running wolf study in North America. Researchers began monitoring their populations in Yukon-Charley Rivers in 1993. In October 2005, the project was incorporated into the National Park Service's Central Alaska Inventory and Monitoring Network. The network is comprised of Denali National Park and Preserve, Wrangell–St. Elias National Park and Preserve, and Yukon-Charley Rivers National Preserve. The three parks collect information on plants, animals, water, and climate and how they interact. The network takes a holistic view of ecosystems, tracking the major physical drivers of ecosystem change and the responses of the two major components of the biota: plants and animals. It has identified fauna distribution and abundance as one of its top three vital signs. In general, the network strives to identify where animals are distributed across the landscape and to track changes in both their distribution and abundance. Species-monitoring efforts include a wide range of vertebrates in network parks, including species of special interest within each park.

Wolves exist in all three parks and are one of six keystone large mammals in Interior Alaska. They are of great importance to people and the ecosystem as a whole. From a monitoring standpoint, wolves are considered reliable indicators of long-term habitat change within park ecosystems because they depend on healthy populations of large ungulate prey, which in turn respond to vegetation, weather, and other habitat patterns across the entire landscape. As apex predators, wolves can play a key role in influencing prey populations, and in turn their prey's influence on vegetation patterns.

The Yukon-Charley Rivers study is tasked with monitoring the overall health of the wolf population: abundance; reproduction rates; parasites and disease, including six specific pathogens; and threats to prey species. In view of the shifting weather due to climate change, the last goal is of particular interest. Farther south, moose carry huge tick loads that can kill or debilitate them, as well as spread disease. The Yukon River corridor is an obvious route for new species to move into Alaska, meaning Yukon-Charley will likely be the first area in Alaska to observe these changes. In fact, cougars and mule deer have been documented many times in the region since 2015. The first moose study in Yukon-Charley was initiated to collect baseline data on moose movements, diet, and disease patterns. The data will also help inform the wolf study, since the health of the prey population affects the health of the wolf population.

After John Burch retired in July 2017, wildlife biologist Mat Sorum became the Yukon-Charley Rivers Vital Signs Lead. He resumed collaring and tracking the preserve's wolves, focusing on the eight to ten packs in its core, adding to the long-term data collection. As a personal goal, Sorum wants to expand public outreach and educate people about Yukon-Charley

Rivers National Preserve and its importance. "People care about the things they know," he said, "and right now relatively few people know of this remarkable place." Another goal is to understand how wolves interact with the broader ecosystem and how this compares to other wolf populations. Few such studies have collected such consistent data related to the health, survival, pack sizes, and movements of wolves across multiple decades. Biologists hope to leverage this data to learn as much as possible about how apex predators influence the world around them. During Sorum's tenure, he has collaborated on studies related to denning, disease transmission and prevalence, and the impacts of climate change. "The Arctic is ground zero for climate change, and having a long-term wolf dataset will help us understand and predict how wolves and their prey will respond to the change."

Over its decades-long run, the Yukon-Charley study has provided valuable insight into the biology of wolves living in the northern wilderness. "We've learned that Yukon-Charley has exceptional wolf habitat owing to its abundant and diverse prey base, including caribou, moose, Dall sheep, beaver, rodents, hares, and salmon," Sorum said. "Yukon-Charley's wolf population has been a source of wolves for the surrounding area." However, he explained that one study found that the state's predator control program implemented between 2005 and 2018 on lands adjacent to the preserve created a population sink that largely relied on immigration from surrounding areas, despite the prohibition on control activities within the preserve. These findings have important implications for the management of protected areas across North America.

Both wolves and moose are designated "vital signs" of the overall well-being of the Yukon-Charley Rivers Preserve. If these animals are healthy and robust, then so, too, is their habitat, for without it, wildlife cannot thrive. The movements of the Wanderer illustrate the importance of ongoing study. No matter how much we think we know about wildlife, especially wide-ranging animals like wolves, there is always more to surprise us and leave us awed.

Author's Note

I first read of Wolf 258's trek in a short piece written by biologist John Burch for the *Vital Signs Monitoring Network Report*. Not long afterward, a newspaper article in the *Fairbanks News-Miner* publicized the wolf's trek. Although short on information, the news piqued my interest, since I have hiked, rafted, camped, and flown over much of the country that Wolf 258 traversed. It didn't seem possible for a lone wolf to navigate that much wilderness in five and a half months and not run afoul of injury, humans, or other wolves. Here was an epic story, based not only on GPS data from Wolf 258's tracking collar but also on geography, natural history, weather, and related human stories.

One delay after another postponed the writing, while research continued in fits and starts. When my friend Kristine Fister assumed the position of acting superintendent of Yukon-Charley Rivers National Preserve in 2020, an opportunity opened to finish the project. She located relevant files for me and provided access to staff photographs taken during the wolf study.

Biologist John Burch and I met in 1986, when he came to Denali National Park to begin a comprehensive wolf study with colleague Tom Meier under the guidance of L. David Mech. Both men proved to be skilled field biologists, as well as approachable and pleasant. In 1996, Burch took over the Yukon-Charley Rivers National Preserve project and moved to Fairbanks. Now retired and living in Nebraska, Burch patiently answered numerous questions and commented on certain passages. Through Layne Adams and John Burch, I was introduced to biologist Mat Sorum, who provided the critical GPS tracking data that made the book possible. Other National Park Service staff, as well as biologists from the Alaska Department of Fish and Game, provided assistance and reports for me to peruse.

Acknowledgments

This book would not have been possible without the assistance of Mat Sorum, John Burch, and Kris Fister, with additional assistance from Layne Adams, Elizabeth Lenart, Bridget Borg, and Seth McMillan. Donald Arthur, DVM, Kimberlee Beckmen, DVM, Nan Eagleson, Margaret Mac-Cluskie, Lindsay McPherson (Parks Canada), Jack Reakoff, Randy Smith, and Erica Watson also contributed to completion of the project. Special thanks to map maker Jordan Pruszenski. Mat Sorum provided significant input on the project and waded through, and commented on, the first draft. Any misstatements or misinterpretations of events or scientific data are solely the errors of the author.

Kate Rogers, Mountaineers Books editor in chief, supported the project from the get-go and offered valuable insight into the entire process. A special thank you to editor Erin Cusick, whose insights and thoughtful, professional editing shaped the book. Without these two stalwarts, this remarkable story would not have been told with such integrity.

About the Author

Tom Walker is a full-time, award-winning professional photographer and writer specializing in Alaska natural history and wildlife. His work has been published in numerous national, local, and international publications. Walker has worked as a conservation officer, wilderness guide, wildlife technician, log home builder, documentary film advisor, and adjunct professor of journalism and photography.

Walker is the author and photographer of sixteen books and coauthor of four travel books. His natural history writings have been anthologized in several collections. His book *Caribou: Wanderer of the Tundra* won a Benjamin Franklin Book Award in the category of nature and environment. He was awarded the Alaska Conservation Foundation's Daniel Houseberg Lifetime Achievement Award for his still photography. The Alaska Historical Society named him Alaska Historian of the Year for *The Seventymile Kid: The Lost Legacy of Harry Karstens and the First Ascent of Mount McKinley*.

Appointed to the Citizens Advisory Committee for the Alaska Interagency Kodiak Brown Bear Management Team, Walker helped draft the first comprehensive brown bear management plan for the Kodiak Archipelago. That same year, his photographs appeared at the Canadian embassy as part of a traveling photo display entitled Saving the Arctic National Wildlife Refuge.

A resident of Alaska for more than fifty years, Walker lives near Denali National Park.

YOU MAY ALSO LIKE

WILD SHOTS

A Photographer's Life in Alaska

Tom Walker

Memoir by a renowned wildlife
photographer, author, and naturalist

A SHAPE IN THE DARK

Living and Dying with Brown Bears

Bjorn Dihle

A wilderness guide's experiences woven
with historical and contemporary accounts
exploring our relationship with one
of the world's most formidable predators

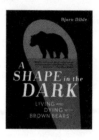

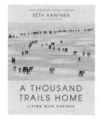

A THOUSAND TRAILS HOME

Living with Caribou

Seth Kantner

Lyrical firsthand account of a life spent hunting,
studying, and living alongside caribou

BELUGA DAYS

Tracking the Endangered White Whale

Nancy Lord

Part personal journey, part exploration of
the challenges this fascinating species faces

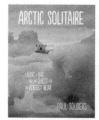

ARCTIC SOLITAIRE

A Boat, a Bay, and the Quest for the Perfect Bear

Paul Souders

The story of a man living out his dream
of photographing the Arctic's most iconic animal, the
polar bear, in its natural habitat